SHARIA VERSUS THE U.S. CONSTITUTION

SHARIA VERSUS THE U.S. CONSTITUTION

WHY AMERICANS MUST CHOOSE FREEDOM

A. S. IBRAHIM

Foreword by
DANIEL A. BRUBAKER

Think and Tell

Published in the United States of America by Think And Tell, LLC, Lovettsville, Virginia.

Think And Tell is committed to publishing books of enduring consequence—works that engage critical questions, including sometimes controversial ones, with honesty and rigor. We believe that truth exists, that it is worth pursuing, and that vigorous and frank discourse is indispensable to that pursuit. The views expressed by published authors do not necessarily represent those of Think And Tell, LLC.

Cover design by Sewwandi Lanaroll. The U.S. Capitol and the Supreme Court building, situated opposite one another on 1st Street NE in Washington, DC, are depicted together on the cover.

ISBN 978-1-949123-38-8 Paperback

ISBN 978-1-949123-39-5 Ebook

Library of Congress Control Number: 2026946061

10 9 8 7 6 5 4 3 2 1

CONTENTS

A NOTE ON TRANSLITERATION

Arabic terms in this book are rendered in simplified form, without the diacritical marks used in academic publications, so that readers unfamiliar with Arabic can engage with them comfortably. Terms that have entered common English usage—such as *sharia*, *hadith*, and *Quran*—are treated as ordinary English words. Less familiar terms are italicized on first appearance and defined in the Glossary. The Appendix uses full scholarly transliteration (following the conventions of the *International Journal of Middle East Studies* (IJMES)) for readers who wish to verify the precise Arabic forms of the principles discussed.

Proper names of historical persons and places follow the most widely recognized English-language spellings rather than strict transliteration—thus *Muhammad* rather than *Muḥammad*, and *Medina* rather than *al-Madīna*—except where a fuller transliteration appears in a direct quotation from a scholarly source.

FOREWORD BY DANIEL A. BRUBAKER

When I was ten, my family moved to Madrid, and the boy who became my closest friend, Ali, lived in our same Pinar de Chamartín apartment building. His family—mother, father, older sister, and baby brother—had reached Spain by a harder road. They had fled the revolution that had just remade Iran, crossing by foot over the mountains into Turkey, carrying what they could and leaving the rest behind. They had reached relative safety. And yet, there in Spain, half a continent from what they had escaped, they still lived in constant fear of being found, and killed.

From Ali and his family I learned something that never left me: how quickly, and how completely, a nation can change when a particular vision of God's law is laid over it—how a family's homeland could become, within months, one they had to flee in the dark. I learned it not from a book but from people I loved and prayed for, by name, every day.

Then they were gone. Not moved, so far as we knew—gone. Their apartment was left as it had been, the furniture in place, as though they had stepped out for an hour and never returned. For many years we did not know whether they had escaped again to somewhere safer, or whether their fears had become reality. For decades I wondered.

In those same years, traveling through that beautiful country, the eyes of this child who loved art were also delighted. I stood in the Alhambra—considering the intricate lacework of its arches, the light moving across the courtyards, and everywhere, carved in stone, flowing Arabic script I could not read. I wondered what the inscriptions said, and about the people who had raised that palace and written those words on its walls: a civilization of aesthetic and architectural competence that had flourished there—and then, centuries before, vanished from Spain.

I did not know, at ten, that those two mysteries—the family who disappeared from our building, and the people who had disappeared from those walls—would shape the course of much of my own life. After 9/11 laid bare the adversity between at least some forms of Islam and American self-government, I spent decades among these texts and histories, seeking to understand how revealed truth (actual or purported), law, power, and the human person fit together—and what it costs when they are arranged one way rather than another.

~

And now, my dear friend Dr. A. S. Ibrahim brings to the question of our time a wisdom born of deep study and lived experience. He grew up in Egypt, where Islamic law shapes both the statute books and the rhythms of daily life—the living reality which I, in my Spanish boyhood, first glimpsed in some of its exiles and architectural vestiges. Following his own formative experiences, Dr. Ibrahim earned two doctorates in Islamic studies, and he now holds the Bill and Connie Jenkins Professorship of Islamic Studies at The Southern Baptist Theological Seminary, with a body of work published by Oxford, Baker Academic, and others. He does not guess at this tradition; he knows it from personal experience followed by disciplined study. And he respects it enough to describe its contours plainly and faithfully.

A scholarly objection is occasionally raised at the threshold of discussions like this one and deserves an answer. Some historians of Islamic law—most notably Wael Hallaq—have argued that *sharia* names no single unified legal system but rather a diverse and decentralized tradition of jurisprudential opinion whose apparent coherence is, in part, a modern construction. The observation has merit as a matter of legal historiography, and Dr. Ibrahim is well aware of it. But it does not reach the argument this book makes. The principles examined here—prescribed death for apostasy and blasphemy, diminished legal standing for women and non-Muslims, the supremacy of Islamic law—appear with striking consistency across the major schools of Islamic jurisprudence—Sunni and Shiʿi alike—over fourteen centuries. These are not contested positions within the classical tradition; they are its settled conclusions. Undergirding all of them is an assumption vigorously asserted but largely unexamined: that Muhammad was a prophet and that the Quran therefore faithfully and finally represents God's will for human governance.

Words from God, if they are words from God, rightly carry weight in the affairs of men. American self-governance, however, embodies a principled humility and restraint on this point—that a claim of divine origin for one scripture among many does not constitute adequate grounds for organizing the coercive legal order of a society that includes those to whom its authenticity has not been demonstrated. And the movements that this book considers do not present themselves as offering one jurisprudential opinion among many possibilities. They present themselves as implementing the law of God—and they are not in the habit of entertaining the epistemological question at all. Whatever diversity exists at the margins of Islamic legal history, it is that claim—of divine supremacy, final and non-negotiable, over any other law—that the American Constitution cannot accommodate. That is what this book examines.

Dr. Ibrahim's unique blend of lived experience, scholarly rigor concerning Islamic sources, and deep appreciation for the United States and her affirmation of individual liberty and its preservation through a wisely designed system of limited self-governance, is what makes this a book that Americans—and others concerned about the advance of Islam in the West, yet unsure what can or should be done—must read. Dr. Ibrahim takes up the question I could only feel as a boy and examines it with scholarly discipline, working through the American constitutional order provision by provision and asking, in each case, how its commitments compare with those of Islamic law as the Quran, the hadith, and centuries of jurisprudence have understood it. Where the two diverge, he shows that the divergence is not a matter of tone that goodwill might smooth away, but a matter of foundations—of what law is, where it comes from, and to whom it finally answers. He looks, too, across the Atlantic, to a Britain and Europe where parallel structures have advanced further than most Americans realize.

One thing I appreciate most about *Sharia Versus the U.S. Constitution* is that it is not an argument against Muslims; it treats a hard subject while keeping a deep respect and love for every person. It is an argument about ideas, and about the systems of law and authority those ideas produce — and it is worth remembering that some of those who understand the weight of such systems most painfully are Muslims themselves. Even from within a broader Islamic cultural framework, Ali's family certainly understood it. They had experienced, in their own lives, the difference between two ways of ordering a society, and they had walked over mountains to put one of them behind them.

Most Americans, we sincerely hope, will never be required to learn that difference the way they did. We were born into the answer. The freedoms we were handed—equal standing before the law, liberty of conscience, the consent of the governed—are not the natural condition of mankind; across the long run of history they are the rare exception, and they do not renew themselves.

It is precisely this order that Dr. Ibrahim weighs against sharia in the pages that follow—and it is worth pausing to see what it rests on. What the American Founders built was neither an accident nor naïveté. It rested on a particular and hard-won wisdom: that legitimate authority in our fallen world rises from the consent of the governed rather than descending from a throne or a clerisy; that power must be divided against itself, checked and balanced, because no single set of human hands can be trusted with all of it; that every person stands equal before laws that are themselves answerable to justice; and that certain rights—to speak, to worship, to follow one's own conscience, to name a few—are granted by no government and so can be revoked by none. They are, in the Founders' words, the endowment of a Creator.

That last conviction is the indispensible hinge of the whole structure. Drawing, with a general reverence, on the Bible and on the bruising political experience of the millennia behind them, the Founders took from both a sober estimate of human nature: that men, being universally sinful, are prone to wrong one another, and prone above all to abuse power, so that a government must be built to restrain not only the governed but the governing. And they grounded the freedom of conscience in a striking premise—that the same Creator who endows us with our rights also leaves us free to accept or reject Him. A God who permits the choice will not be honored by a state that compels it. There, in a sentence, lies the deepest distance between two ways of ordering a society, and much of the reason this book needed to be written in the first place.

None of the foregoing pretends the Founding was without grave fault. It tolerated what it should have abolished and left wrongs in place that cost later generations dearly to undo. But the remarkable thing—the thing worth celebrating without embarrassment—is that the Founders wrote into the nation's charter the very principles that would one day condemn those failures and demand their repair. That all men are created equal was, from the first, a debt the country owed itself; and the long, costly work of paying it—the abolition of slavery and the righting of much else—was accomplished not by abandoning the Founding but by holding it to its word.

This is the inheritance Dr. Ibrahim invites us to see clearly and to weigh. His book offers you a less painful version of what Ali's family experienced tangibly when they left everything behind and crossed those mountains in the dark: a clear understanding of what is truly at stake between these two visions of law and of life—and the chance to act on that understanding while the cost of obtaining it is still little more than the willingness to read and to think—and having thought, perhaps next to speak.

And it arrives at a fitting hour. As the United States mark our two hundred and fiftieth year, we have every reason for gratitude, and—I am convinced—for hope: not the naïve hope that liberty will keep itself, but the well-founded confidence of a free people who, having charted a wiser course than almost any in human history, remain free to choose it again.

The boy who once wondered what had become of his friends who disappeared and what was behind the inscriptions on those old walls in the Alhambra, is honored to place this book in your hands. Read it with your eyes open, and let it help you know how—and why—to choose to preserve freedom.

PREFACE: I HAVE SEEN THIS BEFORE—A WITNESS SPEAKS

I know what sharia looks like. Not from books—though I have read the books, in Arabic, in the original sources, with the training of two PhDs. I know what sharia looks like from the inside. From childhood. From decades of living in a country where its shadow fell across every dimension of daily life—where it shaped who could build what, who could testify against whom, whose daughter could be taken and whose church could be burned, and whose murder would be avenged and whose would be quietly forgotten.

I am a Coptic Christian. I was born in Egypt, grew up in Egypt, and lived in Egypt for more than thirty years before I came to the United States. What I witnessed in those years is not ancient history. It is the living, breathing reality of what happens to a society—to its minorities, its women, its conscience—when Islam becomes the religion of the state and sharia becomes the animating spirit of its legal and cultural life. I did not read about it in a journal article. I lived it. And it is because I lived it that I am writing this book.

THE EGYPT I GREW UP IN

Egypt was not always what it became during my childhood and young adulthood. In earlier generations, Egypt had a cosmopolitan, modernized character—a country that had absorbed European influences, that had a thriving intellectual and cultural life, and in which the different communities that made up its ancient, layered civilization coexisted with a degree of tolerance that, while imperfect, was genuine. That Egypt was already fading by the time I came of age, but its memory was alive enough in the older generations that we understood what was being lost.

What replaced it came with a specific date attached: 1952, when the monarchy was abolished and the Egypt that had gestured toward modernity was replaced by the Egypt of Gamal Abdel Nasser's Arab nationalism. Nasser's relationship with the Islamists was complicated—he suppressed the Muslim Brotherhood when it suited him, but he also opened doors to the Islamist intellectual tradition that could not easily be closed again. His successor, Anwar Sadat, went further, releasing Muslim Brotherhood prisoners from Nasser's jails and allowing Islamist student organizations to flourish on university campuses as a counterweight to leftist movements. Sadat called himself "the believing president." He amended the Egyptian constitution to declare Islam the religion of the state and sharia (Islamic law) a principal source of legislation. He thought he could ride the Islamist tiger. The tiger eventually devoured him—in 1981, at a military parade, in a hail of bullets fired by members of al-Gama'a al-Islamiyya, the Islamic Group, who believed he had not gone far enough.

By then, the Egypt I was growing up in was already transformed. The 1970s and 1980s were the years when Islamist movements—the Muslim Brotherhood, al-Gama'a al-Islamiyya, and the Salafi and Wahhabi movements, flush with oil money pouring in from Saudi Arabia and the Gulf states—consolidated their grip on Egyptian society. The mosques multiplied. The loudspeakers grew louder. Five times a day, the call to prayer was followed, in too many neighborhoods, by sermons that told the faithful what to think about their Christian neighbors. The message was not subtle. Christians were labeled as misguided worshippers of three gods. They were *kuffar* —infidels. They must convert to Islam, pay the *jizya*, or face the consequences that Quran 9:29 prescribed. This demand was not whispered in private. It was broadcast from minarets across the country, day after day, as a matter of religious instruction and public policy simultaneously.

For Copts, those years were years of fear. Christian businesses were set on fire. Christians were murdered. And the government's response—the government of a country whose constitution declared Islam the religion of the state—was weak, evasive, and at times complicit. I remember the massacre of al-Zawiya al-Hamra in 1981, when hundreds of Christians were killed in sectarian violence that the government could not or would not prevent. I remember how the Coptic Pope Shenouda III eventually withdrew to his desert monastery in protest—not a political statement in the ordinary sense, but a profound act of ecclesiastical condemnation, a shepherd refusing to pretend that his flock was safe when it was not.

I remember something else, too. I remember what happened to Muslims who converted to Christianity. They did not face trial. They did not face a formal legal proceeding with charges and evidence and a defense attorney. They simply disappeared—detained in unknown locations, for months or years, without trial, without recourse, without any of the procedural protections that a functioning legal system provides. This is what sharia's apostasy law looks like when it does not dare to name itself officially but operates through the informal mechanisms of a state that takes Islam's supremacy as a given. The constitution may not have said "kill the apostate." But the culture shaped by sharia said it clearly enough that the security services understood their instructions.

I remember the churches. Or rather, I remember the absence of new churches—because building one was effectively impossible. A Coptic community that needed a larger space for worship had to navigate a presidential permission process that could stretch for decades and that was routinely sabotaged at every level. They could not repair a leaking roof. They could not maintain a crumbling wall. They could not fix a bathroom without a government permit that might never come. This obstruction is the *dhimmi* system operating without its classical name—the system that classical sharia prescribes for Christians living under Islamic governance, preserved in the cultural and bureaucratic DNA of a country that had never fully shed its sharia inheritance even as it claimed a modern constitutional identity.

I remember the girls. Coptic girls were kidnapped by Muslim men who knew that the law would be lenient with them—that the social and legal structures of a sharia-informed society would not work with full force to restore a Christian girl who had been "converted" to Islam, however that conversion had been obtained. These situations were not random crimes. They were crimes made possible, and in some cases encouraged, by a legal and cultural environment in which Christians occupied a subordinate status and their victimization carried a reduced legal cost.

This world is what I grew up knowing. It is the world that formed me. And it is the world I carry with me as a witness and as a scholar every time I open the primary sources of Islamic law and read, in the original Arabic, the jurisprudential rulings that created it.

THE DREAM AND THE WARNING

I came to the United States with a dream that I am not embarrassed to describe as American in the fullest sense of the word. I had watched, on a small television screen in Egypt, a television show called *Little House on the Prairie*—a simple American drama about simple American life in which people prayed before their meals without fear, helped their neighbors without calculation, and lived with a dignity that was not contingent on their religion or their place in any social hierarchy. That image lodged itself in me with the force of a calling. I wanted to live in a country where human dignity was not a privilege granted by the powerful to the submissive, but a birthright protected by law.

America gave me that. It gave me more than that. It gave me education—a master's degree, and then two doctoral degrees in Islamic texts and history, earned in the country whose constitutional principles were at odds with the religion I was studying. America gave me the freedom to read the primary sources of Islamic law with a scholar's precision and a survivor's clarity—to know, from the inside of both worlds, what the texts say and what the texts produce when they are applied to human lives. For this country and for everything it has made possible, I am grateful beyond what words adequately express. America is not merely where I live. It is the answer to everything I escaped.

Which is why what I began to see in America filled me with a dread that I recognized immediately, because I had felt it before.

I began to see what to me felt like the organizational infrastructure of the same Islamist movements that had shaped the Egypt of my childhood establishing themselves in American cities. I saw organizations many of whose leaders I perceived to be—if not formally aligned with the Muslim Brotherhood (which I could not determine)—at least sympathetic to its goals and methods operating with remarkable sophistication in the American political and legal environment, advocating for Islamist-friendly policies, supporting Islamist-sympathetic political candidates, and deploying the language of civil rights and religious freedom to advance an agenda whose ultimate goal is anything but civil rights and religious freedom as Americans understand them. I watched fundraising campaigns spread across the country—not for charitable works in the conventional sense, but for what Islamists call their *dawah* (Islamic outreach and proselytization) empire: the acquisition of buildings, the establishment of institutions, the patient construction of an organizational presence designed to normalize Islam's political ambitions in American society.

I saw Islamist organizations seeking out old church buildings—closing congregations, structures that had once been filled with Christian worship—and converting them into mosques or Islamic centers. This conversion is not an innocent real estate transaction. In the symbolic vocabulary of classical Islam, the transformation of a Christian space into an Islamic one is a statement about whose God is ascendant. It is the dawah made architectural. I saw Islamists organize corporate Ramadan prayers in Times Square—not because there were no mosques available in New York City, where hundreds exist, but because the public square is a statement, and occupying it is a claim.

I recognized this pattern. I had seen its earlier, less polished version in Egypt and many other countries in the Middle East. The loudspeakers. The organizational expansion. The slow transformation of public space into Islamic space. The normalization, increment by increment, of the assumption that Islam's requirements take precedence over the arrangements of everyone else.

THE DOUBLE DISCOURSE

What made the American version of this project more sophisticated—and in some ways more dangerous—than what I had witnessed in Egypt was its mastery of double discourse.

In Egypt, the Islamists did not need to hide what they wanted. The cultural and constitutional environment was permissive enough that they could say, from the mosque loudspeaker, exactly what they thought about Christians, about apostates, about the *jizya*, about the proper role of Islamic law in governance. They did not need a public relations strategy because they did not face a constitutional framework designed to resist them.

In America, they do. And so they have developed one—a presentation of

Islam and sharia, offered to American audiences, that diverges sharply from what the classical sources actually say—a gap any reader can verify by setting the reassuring public summaries beside the primary texts themselves. To Americans, they present a version of Islam that is feminist, pluralistic, tolerant, and entirely compatible with constitutional values and Western norms. Muhammad was a champion of women's rights. Islam has always supported religious freedom. Sharia is merely a personal spiritual code, like keeping kosher. There is nothing to see here. Anyone who suggests otherwise is a bigot.

But this *newly invented* Islam bears no relationship to the classical texts. It requires ignoring or falsifying fourteen centuries of history and jurisprudence. It requires pretending that Muhammad's command to kill the apostate does not exist, that the Quran's instruction to collect the *jizya* until the Christian "feels himself humiliated" was a metaphor, that the *hudud* punishments were cultural artifacts rather than Islam's divine mandates, and that the unanimous ruling of every major classical school of Islamic jurisprudence on the legal inferiority of non-Muslims was a misunderstanding.

The double discourse goes further still. I have watched Islamist organizations (which in their classical theological commitments regard homosexuality as a capital offense) publicly align themselves with gay rights movements—not because they have genuinely reformed their theology, but because the political alliance is tactically useful. The Muslim Brotherhood's own strategic documents—available in translation as a matter of public record—describe a patient, incremental approach: advancing Islamist aims through lawful and cultural means rather than open confrontation, building influence first and pressing for doctrine later. I rest the point on that documented strategy rather than on any claim about private intentions—it is the movement's own stated method, and it deserves to be read alongside the classical doctrines this book documents. Ironically, sharia itself justifies this tactic. It includes a well-known legal principle that 'necessity makes permissible that which is forbidden'—in Arabic, *al-darurat tubih al-mahzurat.* In other words, actions that would normally be prohibited become temporarily allowable if they serve to advance or protect Islam.

This façade is the new Islam they are inventing for Western consumption: an Islam distanced from its own classical sources, built not on what Muhammad said and did but on what the target audience wants to hear. Muhammad the feminist. Islam 'the champion of gay rights.' Sharia the personal spiritual code. The classical texts are inconvenient, so they are explained away, recontextualized, mistranslated, or simply ignored—with the confident assumption that Western audiences will not know enough Arabic or enough Islamic jurisprudence to check.

I know enough Arabic. I know enough Islamic jurisprudence. And I am not willing to let the double discourse go unchallenged.

THE QUESTIONS THAT MUST BE ANSWERED

If Islamist organizations in America genuinely want to advance sharia, they owe Americans honest answers to serious questions—not the diplomatic, audience-tested answers they offer in congressional hearings and interfaith dialogues, but the answers that the classical texts actually provide.

What is the status of women under classical sharia—in court testimony, in inheritance, in marriage, in the right to hold political authority? What does *kufr*—infidelity—mean in Islamic law, and how does it affect the legal standing of Christians and Jews? Are Christians and Jews honored as People of the Book, as Western apologists suggest, or are they *kuffar*—infidels—whose toleration is conditional on their submission and their payment of the *jizya*? Under classical sharia, can a non-Muslim testify against a Muslim in court? Can a Christian be a judge? Can a non-Muslim hold authority over Muslims—given the classical principle, stated plainly in Arabic, *La wilaya li-ghayr al-Muslim ala al-Muslim*: no authority for a non-Muslim over a Muslim? Under classical sharia, can Christians freely build churches in Muslim lands—say, in Mecca? Can Muslims seize Christian property? Was the sex slavery of Yazidi women practiced by ISIS a legitimate application of sharia, or an aberration—and if an aberration, on what classical jurisprudential basis?

These issues are not marginal or trick questions. They are the questions that any honest examination of the primary sources answers clearly. The answers are in this book, documented from the sources themselves, in the jurisprudential tradition that Islamist movements cite as their authority. Americans deserve to know those answers. The women, the Christians, the Jews, the gay and lesbian citizens, the former Muslims, and all the other Americans whose constitutional rights would be affected by the imposition of sharia deserve to know exactly what that imposition would mean for them.

WHY I WROTE THIS BOOK

I wrote this book because I have seen what sharia-informed governance produces, and I love this country too much to watch it happen here without raising my voice.

I wrote it because the academic training America gave me—in the primary Arabic sources of Islamic law and history—is precisely the training needed to cut through the double discourse and examine what the texts say. I did not earn two PhDs in Islamic texts and history to remain silent when those texts are being systematically misrepresented to the American public by organizations with a documented political agenda.

I wrote it because I am a Coptic Christian who has lived the dhimmi experience—not as a historical abstraction but as a daily reality—and who therefore cannot pretend that the dhimmi system is an ancient artifact with no contemporary relevance when I have watched it operate in my own lifetime, in my own country, against my own people.

I wrote it because I believe in this country with the intensity of someone who came to it from outside, who dreamed of it before he lived in it, and who knows from personal experience what the alternative looks like.

And I wrote it because the Americans I have met—ordinary, decent, freedom-loving Americans who are beginning to sense that something is wrong, who have heard the word "sharia" and want to understand what it actually means—deserve a clear, honest, source-based account written by someone who has read the primary texts, lived under sharia's cultural influence, and built a life in the constitutional order that sharia seeks to replace.

This book is for them. It is for every American who loves this country and believes that its constitutional principles are worth understanding clearly enough to defend honestly. It is for all the former Muslims living in America who practice their new faith or their new freedom in quiet fear of communities that have not left the classical texts behind. It is for every Christian and Jewish American who does not know that classical sharia has a specific legal category—dhimmi—designed precisely for them, with specific sociopolitical and legal disabilities attached to it. It is for every woman who does not know that Islamic jurisprudence assigns her testimony in court a value half that of a man's. And it is for every gay and lesbian American who does not know that the legal tradition being advanced by Islamist organizations in their country prescribes their death.

They deserve to know. Knowledge is not hostility or bigotry. It is the precondition of defense.

A FINAL WORD BEFORE WE BEGIN

This book is written with genuine respect for Muslim people—for neighbors, colleagues, and friends whose personal decency and genuine faith I have seen at close range. I do not write this book in anger, though I have had reasons for anger. I write it in the conviction that truth, stated clearly and grounded in primary sources, is the most powerful tool that free people possess—and that silence in the face of a documented threat to constitutional freedom is not tolerance. It is abdication.

America gave me everything. The education. The freedom. The dignity that my country of birth could not consistently provide. The constitutional order that does not ask me, on the way to the courthouse, whether I am Muslim or Christian, whether I am a man or a woman, whether I have paid my *jizya* and accepted my subordination.

I owe this country my honest witness. This book is that witness—offered with gratitude, with scholarly rigor, and with the heartfelt conviction that what America has built is worth defending with every honest word at our disposal.

The pages that follow are those words. Let us begin.

A.S. Ibrahim, Kentucky, April 2026

INTRODUCTION: THE LAW SOME PREFER YOU DON'T READ

There is a conversation happening in America that many people are afraid to have. It involves a legal and political system that billions of people consider sacred, that governs the daily lives of Muslims in dozens of countries around the world, that has been in open conflict with Western democratic values for decades—and that a growing number of Americans are only now beginning to understand. That system is called sharia.

For years, any serious discussion of sharia in the West was dismissed as bigotry, conflated with hatred of Muslims as people, or buried under so many academic qualifications that ordinary citizens gave up trying to understand it. The subject became politically radioactive. Critics were shouted down. Journalists changed the subject. And while the conversation was being suppressed in polite society, sharia was being discussed quite openly—and promoted quite deliberately—in mosques, university lecture halls, and the corridors of political advocacy organizations across the United States.

That silence is ending. Americans are paying attention.

A NATION WAKING UP

Interest in "sharia law," according to Google search trends in the United States, surged in late 2025, after years of relative dormancy. It has not subsided. Across the country, from school board meetings to congressional hearings, from church pulpits to state legislatures, Americans are asking the same urgent question: What exactly is sharia, and does it pose a threat to the way we live?

The legislative response has been substantial. As of 2026, a growing number of states—including Alabama, Arizona, Florida, Kansas, Louisiana, North Carolina, South Dakota, Texas, and Tennessee—have enacted legislation banning or restricting the application of sharia in their courts. These laws vary in language and scope, but they share a common concern: that a foreign legal system, rooted in Islamic doctrine rather than popular consent, should never be permitted to override the constitutional rights of American citizens.

The movement has reached Congress as well. In 2025, members of the House of Representatives introduced the "Preserving a sharia-Free America Act," seeking to amend the Immigration and Nationality Act to prohibit the entry of aliens who adhere to sharia law. A "Sharia-Free America" caucus in the House has surged to over fifty members, with lawmakers from Texas and Florida making up more than a third of its membership.

Meanwhile, polling data have added another dimension to the debate. A recent survey found that 39 percent of American Muslims support the implementation of sharia law in the United States—compared to only 10 percent of the general public. By contrast, 56 percent of the general public opposed it outright. Whatever one makes of these numbers, they reveal something important: sharia is not a fringe issue, and the concerns Americans have about it are not manufactured hysteria. They are a rational response to a real question about the future of this country's constitutional order.

This book is an attempt to answer that question—honestly, specifically, and without apology.

WHAT IS SHARIA?

Part of the problem is that most Americans, when they hear the word "sharia," have no concrete idea what they are dealing with. They may have a vague sense that it involves harsh punishments or the oppression of women. They may have heard Muslim advocates insist that sharia is simply "a personal moral code" or "the Muslim version of keeping kosher." They may have been told by well-meaning professors that sharia is endlessly diverse and subject to interpretation, making any generalization meaningless.

All these framings have an element of truth. But all of them, taken alone, obscure far more than they reveal.

The word *sharia* in Arabic means a "straight path"—the path of divine guidance as Allah revealed it through Muhammad. But sharia is not a book. It is not a single document you can read cover to cover. Its rules and principles are drawn from multiple sources considered sacred by the Muslim community—chiefly the Quran, the word of Allah as revealed to Muhammad, and the Hadith, the recorded sayings and deeds of Muhammad himself. Whatever Muhammad said or did is, in classical Islamic teaching, considered sacred and mandatory to imitate.

The first concept Americans need to understand is that sharia is not like Christian moral teaching, which addresses the soul and leaves civil governance to secular institutions. Sharia is a comprehensive and uncompromising political and legal order. It was designed not only to govern a believer's private relationship with Allah, but to regulate courts, criminal penalties, warfare, governance, commerce, marriage, the treatment of women, and the legal status of non-Muslims. There is no equivalent in Western religious traditions.

The second aspect Americans need to understand is who has the authority to interpret sharia. Most Muslims—even devout ones—are not scholars of Islamic law. They depend entirely on religious leaders to tell them what sharia requires. This situation invests enormous power in the hands of those scholars and institutions, and it means that the version of sharia being promoted in any given mosque, classroom, or political organization is only as moderate or radical as the theology of the men doing the promoting.

RELIGION OR POLITICAL POWER? ISLAM INSISTS IT IS BOTH

Here is where many well-intentioned Americans make a serious mistake. They look at sharia through the lens of Western religious experience—through the tradition of the Reformation, of church-state separation, of faith as a private matter between the individual and God. By that lens, sharia looks like a religious code, and therefore something the First Amendment's religious freedom protections should place beyond criticism.

That lens is wrong—not because critics say so, but because Islam's own primary sources say so.

In classical Islamic teaching, nothing in Islam is exclusively religious. Islam is understood as both religion and political power—it encompasses worship as well as political leadership, spiritual life as well as governance and law. The rationale runs directly from the life of Muhammad himself. He was not only a prophet; he was a military commander, a judge, a lawgiver, and the ruler of a political community who established his authority through military conquest. If Muhammad embodied both religious and political leadership, then—in Islamic reasoning—the two cannot be separated. Politics is not incidental to Islam; it is essential to it.

The result is a legal system that governs virtually every dimension of human life. Sharia defines how a Muslim worships Allah and how a Muslim treats fellow human beings. It dictates how to deal with other Muslims, how to conduct commerce, how to marry and divorce, and—critically—how to treat people who are not Muslims. That last category is where sharia's conflict with the American constitutional order becomes most concrete and most alarming.

ISLAM IN AMERICA: THE DISTINCTION THAT CANNOT BE OVERLOOKED

Before going further, a distinction must be made—one that is foundational to every argument in this book.

There is a difference between Muslims and Islamism.

Millions of Muslims in America are exactly what they appear to be: ordinary people, neighbors, citizens, who pray, fast, raise families, and have no front-of-mind intention to impose any legal system on anyone. The Constitution protects their right to live that way, and nothing in this book challenges it. Individual Muslims deserve the full protection of American law and the respect of their fellow citizens.

Islamism is something else. It is the political ideology that takes sharia out of the mosque and into the courts, the legislature, the university, and the public square. It seeks to establish Islamic law as governing law—not as a personal practice, but as a social and political order. Islamists understand that in America, this project cannot be pursued through military conquest. It is pursued instead through legal strategy, political alliance, academic influence, and the patient exploitation of the very freedoms that American democracy provides.

The growth of Islamist influence in the United States is not a conspiracy theory. It is documented, deliberate, and ongoing. After September 11, 2001, many voices—especially on the political left—began reflexively defending Islam from any criticism, in part as a reaction against the excesses of the post-9/11 "war on terror." Islamist organizations were quick to exploit this dynamic. They aligned themselves with progressive political movements, presenting Muhammad's values as compatible with—even identical to—liberal values of diversity and inclusion. The alignment is, upon any serious examination, a profound contradiction. But it has been politically effective.

Meanwhile, wealthy Islamist states—most notably Qatar and Saudi Arabia—have invested hundreds of millions of dollars in American universities, funding endowed academic chairs and research centers designed to shape how Islam and sharia are taught and discussed in the institutions that train America's future leaders, lawyers, and journalists. The result is a generation of opinion-shapers who have been told, systematically, that sharia is benign, that concerns about it are rooted in bigotry, and that anyone who raises the subject seriously is motivated by hatred rather than by concern for constitutional principles.

This book rejects that framing. It does so not out of hostility to Muslims, but out of fidelity to the facts—facts drawn from sharia's own primary sources, in Arabic, as classical Islamic jurisprudence has understood and applied them for over a thousand years.

A SHORT DICTIONARY FOR THE ROAD AHEAD

Several potentially unfamiliar terms appear throughout the chapters that follow. Six deserve clear definitions upfront, because they are often misused—both by those who fear sharia and by those who defend it. For easy reference, there is a full glossary of these and other technical terms at the back of the book.

Sharia is Islamic divine law, derived from the Quran and the Hadith (Muhammad's teachings and traditions), governing all aspects of Muslim religious life and, in its classical form, all aspects of political and civil society as well. Sharia is not a single book, but a body of legal rulings accumulated over centuries.

Fiqh is the human science of interpreting sharia—Islamic jurisprudence. If sharia is divine law in principle, *fiqh* is the work of Muslim legal scholars who articulate and translate that law into practical rulings. Several distinct schools of *fiqh* developed over the centuries, each with its own interpretive tradition. When this book refers to "classical sharia," it refers to the rulings of these established schools, not to any individual's private interpretation.

Hudud refers to a specific category of punishments prescribed in the Quran and Hadith, with fixed penalties that human judges are not free to reduce or set aside. These include amputation of hands for theft, flogging for certain sexual offenses, and death for apostasy—leaving Islam—and adultery. These are not ancient relics. They are applied as law in multiple countries today. These are repeatedly applied in countries that apply the sharia (e.g., the Taliban in Afghanistan).

Dhimmi is the legal Muslim category that classical Sharia assigns to Christians and Jews living under Islamic governance. The term stigmatizes minorities and carries the meaning of "protected"—but that protection is conditional and profoundly unequal. The term derives from the Arabic root dh-m-m, meaning "to vilify," "to disparage," or, in other contexts, "to blame," signifying a compact whose breaking necessitates blame. The dhimmi is thus not merely a "protected person" but someone living under perpetual threat of disparagement and blame, and their legal consequences, with no reciprocal enforcement mechanism against Muslims who violated their obligations. In practice, dhimmis paid the *jizya*—a poll tax collected with deliberate ritual humiliation, mandated by Quran 9:29 until the non-Muslim feels humiliated and subdued. Based on this status, dhimmis were forbidden from building churches, praying openly, holding authority over Muslims, bearing arms, or displaying their faith publicly. For many classical Muslim jurists, the purpose of the dhimmi system is the exaltation of Islam and the humiliation of unbelief. This is institutionalized second-class status, not tolerance.

Umma is the global community of all Muslims, transcending national borders and citizenship. In Islamist political thinking, loyalty to the umma supersedes loyalty to any earthly state or constitution.

Islamism, as distinct from personal Islamic faith, is the political ideology that seeks to make sharia the governing law of society. Not all Muslims are Islamists. But Islamism is an organized, well-funded, and strategically sophisticated movement—and it is the subject of this book's concern.

THE ARGUMENT, PLAINLY STATED

Sharia—in its classical, authoritative form, as derived from the Quran, the Hadith, and the accumulated rulings of Islamic jurisprudence—is a legal and political order that is fundamentally incompatible with the United States Constitution. This distinction is not a matter of cultural preference or religious prejudice. It is a matter of direct, specific, point-by-point conflict.

The chapters that follow trace that conflict across the full architecture of American constitutional law. **Chapter One** shows how sharia's demand for divine supremacy over all governance violates the First Amendment's Establishment Clause and the foundational American principle of the prohibition of government establishing a religion. **Chapter Two** examines Islam's death penalty for apostasy and its collision with the First Amendment's absolute protection of religious freedom. **Chapter Three** addresses sharia's blasphemy laws—the criminalization of any criticism of Muhammad or the Quran—and their irreconcilable conflict with free speech. **Chapter Four** documents the legal hierarchy sharia imposes on non-Muslims: the dhimmi system, with its unequal blood money, its exclusion from court testimony, its subjugation taxes, its prohibition on building churches—a system that violates, at every point, the Fourteenth Amendment's guarantee of equal protection under the law. **Chapter Five** examines sharia's prescribed physical punishments—amputation, stoning, flogging—and their conflict with the Eighth Amendment's prohibition on cruel and unusual punishment. **Chapter Six** confronts the deepest incompatibility of all: sharia's location of ultimate sovereignty in Allah and his jurists, directly opposing the Constitution's bedrock principle that legitimate authority derives from the consent of the governed. **Chapter Seven** addresses the question of accommodation—why sharia cannot be treated as simply another form of private religious practice, and why the Constitution's protections for religious freedom do not extend to the enforcement of a parallel political-legal system.

Americans of goodwill disagree about many things. But the constitutional principles at stake here—freedom of religion, freedom of speech, equal protection under law, popular sovereignty, the prohibition of state-established religion—are not matters of partisan dispute. They are the shared inheritance of every American, regardless of party, background, or faith. Understanding what threatens them is the first step toward defending them.

That is what this book is for.

1

ONE NATION UNDER ALLAH—WHY SHARIA AND THE FIRST AMENDMENT CANNOT COEXIST

Open any American civics textbook and you will find, somewhere near the beginning, a sentence that generations of schoolchildren have memorized without fully appreciating its radicalism: Congress shall make no law respecting an establishment of religion. Ten words into the First Amendment, the Founders drew the most consequential boundary in the history of democratic governance. The government of the United States will not be the special instrument of any church, scripture, or clergy. The people govern themselves. The law belongs to the people.

That sentence is not just a legal rule. It is a statement about the nature of legitimate authority. In America, laws derive their power from the consent of the governed—from elections, legislatures, courts, and a Constitution that can be amended by human beings. No divine mandate, no prophetic decree, no religious text has the force of American law simply because it claims to come from God.

Sharia disagrees—not partially, nor in some interpretations, but in its classical and authoritative form—the form that Islamist movements reference, promote, and seek to implement—sharia disagrees completely. It holds that Allah alone is the sovereign, that his law alone is legitimate, and that any human system of governance that does not derive its authority from his divine revelation is, by definition, a form of infidelity and idolatry.

That is not a clash of cultures. It is a clash of constitutions.

THE GOVERNMENT THAT ALLAH BUILT

To understand why sharia cannot coexist with the First Amendment's Establishment Clause, you first need to understand what sharia claims to be.

In classical Islamic theology, the concept that governs all political life is called *hakimiyya*—divine sovereignty. The word comes from the Arabic root meaning "to govern" or "to judge," and in the Islamic tradition it is applied exclusively to Allah. Allah alone governs. Allah alone judges. Allah alone has the right to make law. This claim is not a metaphor or a spiritual sentiment. This is an Islamic constitutional principle—one rooted in Quranic verses that Islamic legal scholars have interpreted and elaborated across fourteen centuries, and that twentieth-century Islamist theorists, above all Mawdudi and Qutb, systematized into an explicit political doctrine with direct implications for democratic governance.

In verse after verse, the Quran makes explicit the illegitimacy of any human government that disagrees with it. In Surah 12:40, the Quran declares: "Legislation [or judgement, Arabic, *al-ḥukm*] belongs only to Allah." In Surah 5:44, it warns: "Those who do not judge by what Allah has revealed are the infidels." In Surah 4:65, it states that a Muslim cannot truly believe "until he makes you the judge in all disagreements and finds no resistance in his heart to your rulings"—where "you" is understood to be reference to Muhammad, whose rulings are considered an extension of divine law, because he is viewed as the best human model of applying Allah's sharia. These are not obscure passages cherry-picked from the margins. They are foundational texts that Islamic legal scholars have cited for over a thousand years to establish that governance and legislation are, by divine command, a religious function.

Muhammad himself understood his role this way. He was not merely a preacher delivering spiritual guidance. He was a head of state who enacted laws, commanded armies, judged disputes, ordered executions, negotiated treaties, and established a political community in which religious authority and political authority were one and the same. The city of Medina under Muhammad was history's first Islamic state—and it was governed by divine command, not popular consent.

These truths are why, in classical sharia, there is no such thing as "man-made law" that possesses genuine legitimacy. Human legislation—including the United States Constitution—is regarded, in this framework, as a usurpation of Allah's authority. Islamic legal scholars use the term *tughyan*—tyranny or transgression—to describe governance that does not derive from divine law. A democracy in which human beings vote on their own laws is *not*, in this view, a legitimate form of government. It is a form of collective rebellion against Allah.

NOT A PRIVATE FAITH—A GOVERNING ORDER

At this point, a reasonable American might object: But don't we have millions of Muslim citizens who live peacefully under the Constitution without any apparent desire to overthrow it? Don't most Muslims in America simply practice their faith privately, go to work, raise their children, and leave their neighbors alone?

Yes. And this book is not about them.

But here is the distinction that matters, and that Islamist advocates work very hard to prevent Americans from making clearly. There is a difference between how individual Muslims choose to live and what sharia, in its classical form, demands. Many Christians do not observe every teaching of their church or scripture. Many Jews do not keep kosher. Personal practice and doctrinal requirements are not the same thing. When we are evaluating whether sharia is compatible with the Constitution, we are not asking how each individual Muslim lives. We are asking what sharia, in its authoritative sources and classical jurisprudence, actually requires—because those requirements are what Islamist supporters, groups, and movements seek to implement.

And what sharia requires, in those sources, is not mere personal piety. It is total governance.

Sharia regulates prayer—but also criminal punishment. It addresses fasting—but also the rules of warfare. It guides marital life—but also the legal status of non-Muslims in court. It speaks to the inner life of the soul—but also to who may hold political authority over whom. It claims Allah created all—but also dictates how men are superior to women and guardians over them. There is no domain of human life that classical sharia leaves to secular governance. This assertion is not a Western critic's caricature of Islam. It is what Islamic scholars themselves have consistently taught.

The great medieval jurist Ibn Taymiyya explained clearly that the purpose of political authority is the implementation of religion. The twentieth-century Islamist theorist Sayyid Qutb—whose writings continue to influence Islamist movements worldwide—was blunter still: any society that does not govern by Allah's law is a society in a state of *jahiliyya*, the Arabic term for pre-Islamic barbarism and ignorance. That includes, explicitly, Western democracies, about which Qutb was writing.

This tension is the heart of the incompatibility. The First Amendment's Establishment Clause was written to prevent precisely this scenario: the fusion of religious authority with state power. The Founders had seen what state-established religion looked like in Europe—the religious wars, the persecution of dissenters, the coercion of conscience—and they were determined that the American republic would never become a dedicated instrument of any church, any creed, or of God's claimed representatives on earth. Sharia, as Muslim jurists conveyed for centuries, is not a private faith seeking only to be left alone. It is a governing system that claims the right—and bears the obligation—to replace any other law with divine law wherever it achieves the power to do so.

"WE DON'T ACCEPT MAN-MADE LAWS"

The statement, "We do not accept manmade laws" is not theoretical. You can hear it said openly, in American mosques, on American university campuses, and in countless conversations online.

In 2015, a Muslim scholar addressing a gathering in the United States was asked whether American Muslims could fully accept the Constitution as their governing law. His answer was unambiguous: a Muslim cannot regard any law as supreme except Allah's law. The Constitution, he said, might be followed provisionally—as a matter of practical necessity—but it could never be accepted as *legitimate* in the way sharia is legitimate, because legitimacy, in Islam, belongs to Allah alone.

This position is not the eccentric view of one radical preacher. It reflects a substantial body of classical Islamic legal opinion. The concept of *dar al-harb*—literally "the house of war"—is the classical Islamic designation for territories not governed by sharia. A Muslim living in *dar al-harb* (and this term describes the United States, among others) is living under a fundamentally illegitimate order. The obligation of the Muslim community, over time, is to transform *dar al-harb* into *dar al-Islam*—the house of Islam, governed by sharia. That transformation, in different schools of thought and different historical moments, has been achieved through military conquest, through missionary expansion, and through the patient, long-term strategy of political and cultural influence that Islamist movements in the West are pursuing today.

Browse the social media pages of Islamist organizations operating in the United States and you will find this language used without embarrassment. "Sharia is the only law we need." "Democracy is *shirk*"—*shirk* being the Islamic term for the gravest sin: worshipping something other than Allah. "The Constitution was written by men; the Quran was written by Allah." These lines are not fringe comments. They reflect a coherent theological position that has deep roots in Islamic legal thought and that Islamist groups articulate openly to their members while presenting a very different face to the broader American public.

HOW THE STRATEGY WORKS

The genius—and the danger—of the Islamist approach in America is that it uses the First Amendment to advance a system that would ultimately destroy the First Amendment.

Here is how it works in practice. An Islamist organization—say, a mosque, a student group, or a political advocacy organization—invokes the Free Exercise Clause to demand that its religious practices be accommodated. Such accommodation is entirely appropriate. The First Amendment protects the practice of religion and the exercise of conscience. But the same organization then uses that protected status as a platform to advance sharia-compatible positions in law, politics, and public culture—arguing, for instance, that criticism of Islam should be restricted as "hate speech," that sharia arbitration panels should be recognized by civil courts, or that public institutions should adopt policies that reflect Islamic norms.

Many of these individual steps look, in isolation, like the reasonable exercise of religious freedom. Taken together, they constitute a project of incremental legal and cultural transformation—one that operates entirely within the language of American constitutional rights while working steadily toward a goal that those constitutional rights were designed to prevent: the establishment of a sectarian religious legal order.

This scenario is not speculation. It is the explicit strategic vision that has been documented in the founding charters of major Islamist organizations, in the writings of their intellectual leaders, and in court documents from federal prosecutions. The Muslim Brotherhood—the grandfather organization of Islamist movements worldwide—described its mission in America in a 1991 internal document as "a kind of grand jihad in eliminating and destroying the Western civilization from within and 'sabotaging' its miserable house by their hands and the hands of the believers so that it is eliminated and God's religion is made victorious over all other religions." The strategy is patient, sophisticated, and long-term. And it depends, at every stage, on Americans failing to understand the difference between Islam as a personal faith and Islamism as a political project.

If Islam is viewed *solely* as a religion, Americans may be disarmed by their own commitment to religious freedom. Islam, however, is not only a religion; it is also a conquering ideology. It requires hegemony and superiority over every other political and religious system. Sharia, as a political-religious system, is fundamentally anti-American on multiple levels.

THE ESTABLISHMENT CLAUSE WAS MADE FOR SUCH A SITUATION

The American Founders did not write the Establishment Clause as mere abstraction. They wrote it from experience—bitter, lived experience of what happens when religious institutions capture political power. They had studied the history of Europe's religious wars. They had seen the Church of England's coercive authority. They had felt, in their own colonies, the weight of religious establishments that taxed, persecuted, and disenfranchised those who did not conform.

The Baptist tradition in early America was particularly insistent on this point. Roger Williams, founder of Rhode Island, argued that coercing religious conscience was a sin against both God and man. John Leland, the Baptist minister who lobbied James Madison to include religious freedom protections in the Bill of Rights, believed that soul freedom—the right of every human being to follow his own conscience before God without state interference—was the most sacred political principle a free society could enshrine.

What Leland and Madison understood—and what their Establishment

Clause enshrined—was that the moment a government makes any religious system the exclusive basis of its law, it begins to coerce the conscience of everyone who does not share that religion. It doesn't matter whether the religion is Christianity, Judaism, or Islam. State-established religion is incompatible with human freedom. The Establishment Clause protects Muslims in America from a Christian theocracy. By the same logic—indeed, by the same clause—it protects Christians, Jews, atheists, and everyone else from a system in which Islamic law becomes the governing authority.

Classical sharia, by its own account, is incompatible with this tradition. It does not offer equal legal standing to other faiths as a matter of principle. It tolerates them—provisionally, conditionally, and under a regime of explicit legal subordination. The *dhimmi* system, which will be examined in detail in Chapter Four, institutionalizes that subordination. But even before we get to the details of dhimmi law, the basic structure of sharia's claim—that Allah's sovereignty supersedes all human law, that the Constitution is a man-made document with no legitimate authority before Allah—is itself a direct challenge to the Establishment Clause.

You cannot have two supreme laws. You cannot have a system in which Allah's command and "We the People" are both the ultimate source of legitimate authority. One must yield to the other. Sharia, in its classical form, is unambiguous about which one should yield—and it is not sharia.

WHAT THE CONSTITUTION PROTECTS—AND WHAT IT CANNOT

The First Amendment protects every Muslim in America just as it protects everyone else. It protects the right to pray five times a day, to fast during Ramadan, to wear a hijab, to build mosques, to preach the faith, to raise children in the tradition of Islam, to organize politically, and to advocate for any position in the public square. These are genuine constitutional rights, and they apply to Muslims exactly as they apply to every other American. No law may abridge them.

What the First Amendment does not protect—what the Establishment Clause specifically prohibits—is the use of state power to enforce religious law as such. Not Christian religious law. Not Jewish religious law. Not Islamic religious law. The moment that sharia moves from the *supposed* personal practice of individual believers into the public enforcement mechanisms of courts, legislatures, police, or government policy, it crosses the line that the Establishment Clause was drawn to hold.

The distinction sounds simple. In practice, it is being tested constantly. When a sharia arbitration panel issues a ruling that violates the constitutional rights of a party—most often a woman in a divorce or custody dispute—and that party seeks enforcement in a civil court, the question is no longer a religious one. It is a constitutional one. When a state institution adopts policies under pressure from Islamist advocacy groups that effectively impose Islamic norms on non-Muslim participants, the Establishment Clause is implicated. When political candidates openly advocate for sharia-compatible legislation as a matter of religious obligation, the boundary between religious freedom and religious establishment is being tested.

Americans have every reason to understand these distinctions clearly, because those who wish to advance sharia in this country depend entirely on Americans failing to make them. They depend on the assumption that raising the issue must be bigotry, that protecting constitutional principles is indistinguishable from hating Muslims, and that the better part of wisdom is to remain silent and look the other way.

This book is not willing to look the other way.

A NATION FOUNDED ON A PRINCIPLE

America was not founded on Christian law, though most of its Founders were Christians. It was not founded on biblical commandments, though many early Americans revered the Bible. It was founded on a principle—the principle that legitimate authority derives from the free consent of free people, and that no church, no scripture, and no claim of divine mandate can override that consent.

That principle is what the Establishment Clause protects. It protects believers of every faith from the coercive power of anyone else's religion. It protects the Muslim American from establishment of a Christian theocracy. It protects the Jewish American from establishment of an evangelical state. And it protects every American—Muslim, Christian, Jewish, secular, and everything in between—from a governing system that declares itself the exclusive instrument of Allah's will, that assigns legal inequality to those who do not share its faith, and that regards the Constitution itself as an illegitimate usurpation of divine sovereignty.

Sharia, in its classical description, is precisely that system. Not because critics say so, but because sharia says so—in its own texts, in its own terms, in the fourteen-hundred-year tradition of Islamic legal scholarship that Islamist movements adopt, cherish, and invoke as their authority.

The First Amendment was built to hold this line. Understanding that we need to hold it—and why—is the beginning of an honest national conversation that is long overdue.

2

YOU CAN CHECK OUT, BUT YOU CAN NEVER LEAVE—ISLAM'S DEATH PENALTY FOR APOSTASY AND THE FIRST AMENDMENT

Imagine waking up one morning and deciding, after years of honest reflection, that you no longer believe what you were raised to believe. Maybe it happened gradually—doubts accumulating quietly over years, questions that never got satisfying answers, a slow but undeniable drift away from the faith of your childhood. Maybe it happened suddenly, the way these things sometimes do. However it happened, you make a decision that is deeply personal, profoundly American, and protected by the very first right enumerated in the Bill of Rights: you change your religion.

In the United States, that decision costs you nothing legally. You may lose some relationships. You may face family heartbreak or social pressure. Those are real and painful consequences. But the government cannot touch you. No court can punish you. No law prescribes a penalty for leaving one faith and joining another, or joining none at all. The First Amendment is absolute on this point: the state has no business in the personal religious choices of free citizens.

Under sharia, that same decision can cost you your life.

This fact is the mainstream, classical, orthodox ruling of every major school of Islamic jurisprudence, grounded in the explicit commands of Muhammad himself, applied by Islamic courts across fourteen centuries of history, and enforced as law in multiple Muslim-majority countries today.

And it represents one of the most direct, irreconcilable conflicts between sharia and the United States Constitution.

MUHAMMAD'S COMMAND

Muhammad's ruling on apostasy is among the most clearly documented in all of Islamic tradition. The source material is unambiguous: a Muslim who leaves Islam forfeits his right to live.

The hadith—the recorded sayings and actions of Muhammad, which carry binding legal authority in classical sharia—states the matter in five words. Recorded in *Sahih al-Bukhari*, the most authoritative hadith collection in Sunni Islam, Muhammad declared: "Whoever changes his Islamic religion, kill him." This is not a dubious statement buried in an obscure text. *Sahih al-Bukhari* is to Islamic jurisprudence what the Supreme Court Reporter is to American law—the gold standard, the authoritative record, cited by scholars across every major school of Islamic legal thought for over a thousand years. The hadith is classified among Muslim scholars as *sahih*—sound, authentic, verified, and reliable. If critical western scholars may be skeptic about ancient texts, Muslim scholars do not dispute that Muhammad said it precisely as written.

Muhammad did not merely issue this ruling as an abstract legal principle. He acted on it. In his biography and in the historical record of early Islam, there are documented cases of individuals who left Islam and faced lethal consequences. When a group of men from the tribe of Ukl came to Medina, embraced Islam, then abandoned it, Muhammad's response—recorded in *Sahih al-Bukhari*—was to pursue them, cut off their hands and feet, and gouge out their eyes with heated nails before leaving them to die in the desert. The narration is graphic precisely because it is meant to be: it establishes, beyond any reasonable doubt, that the penalty for apostasy was annihilation. To classical Muslim jurists, who are regarded by Muslims as pious and authoritative, Muhammad's actions are prescriptive, not descriptive.

In another well-documented case from the early Islamic community, a man named Ubaydallah ibn Jahsh and others who had converted to Christianity after previously embracing Islam were considered to have placed themselves outside the protection of the Muslim community—a legal status that, in classical sharia, carries grave consequences. The principle was established early and maintained consistently: a Muslim who abandons Islam forfeits the legal protections that Islam affords.

The pattern did not end with Muhammad's death. In the immediate aftermath, during the *Ridda* Wars (Wars of Apostasy), the first caliph, Abu Bakr, launched military campaigns against Arabian tribes who abandoned Islam or refused to continue their political and financial obligations to Medina. These conflicts were prosecuted as acts of apostasy warranting armed suppression. In this way, the early Muslim leadership reinforced and expanded the precedent that departure from Islam could be met with force, helping to shape the legal and political framework that later jurists would formalize into doctrines on apostasy.

WHAT THE SCHOLARS SAID—FOR A THOUSAND YEARS

Muhammad's command did not remain an isolated incident. It became the cornerstone of Islamic apostasy law, elaborated and systematized by the well-known and highly regarded jurists of every major school of Sunni and Shiʿi legal thought across a thousand years of scholarship.

The four major Sunni schools of jurisprudence—Hanafi, Maliki, Shafiʾi, and Hanbali—all prescribe death as the penalty for apostasy, with variations only on procedural details. The Hanafi school, followed predominantly in South Asia and much of the Arab world, specifies a waiting period of three days during which the apostate is given the opportunity to recant, after which, if he refuses, he is to be executed without mercy. Importantly, the Hanafi school holds that a female apostate should be imprisoned and beaten every three days until she returns to Islam rather than executed—not out of leniency toward women, but because classical Hanafi jurists believed a woman's testimony and legal standing were too limited to constitute the same degree of threat to the community. The Maliki, Shafiʾi, and Hanbali schools prescribe death for both male and female apostates.

The Shafiʾi scholar Imam al-Nawawi, one of the most celebrated jurists in Islamic history, wrote plainly in his authoritative manual *Minhaj al-Talibin*: "When a Muslim apostatizes from Islam, the imam asks him to repent. If he repents, well and good. If not, he is killed." There is no hedging there, but only a direct fulfilment of Muhammad's instructions. There is no historical qualification, no note that this judgment applied only to seventh-century Arabia. It is the ruling of a scholar whose legal opinions are considered binding by millions of Muslims to this day.

Ibn Qudama, the great Sunni Hanbali jurist of the twelfth century, was equally direct: "The apostate is to be asked to repent. If he repents, he is released. If he does not, he is killed." Ibn Taymiyya, perhaps the most influential Islamic jurist of the medieval period, affirmed the same ruling and extended it: apostasy, in his view, was the most dangerous crime a person could commit against the Muslim community, because it struck at the foundations of Islamic society itself.

Clearly, this position is not a fringe one held only by extremists. It is the mainstream, classical, orthodox position of Islamic legal scholarship—the *fiqh* that Islamist movements cite as their authority, the *fiqh* that governs apostasy law in countries that operate under sharia today.

IT IS HAPPENING RIGHT NOW

A Western reader might be tempted to place all of the foregoing safely in the past—the medieval world, a different era, practices that modernity has left behind. That temptation should be resisted firmly.

As of today, apostasy is a capital crime under the law of multiple Muslim-majority countries, including Saudi Arabia, Iran, Afghanistan, Qatar, Yemen, and parts of Nigeria and Malaysia. In Saudi Arabia—America's strategic ally in the Middle East, the birthplace of Islam, the custodian of its two holiest Muslim cities—a man who publicly declares that he has left Islam can be charged with apostasy, tried in a sharia court, and sentenced to death. In Iran, the Islamic Republic's penal code treats apostasy as a capital offense. In Afghanistan under Taliban rule, the penalty is death. These are not rogue states applying aberrant interpretations. They are applying sharia as Islamic jurisprudence has always understood it.

The human cost is staggering and ongoing. Consider the case of Meriam Ibrahim, a Sudanese woman who was raised as a Christian by her Christian mother after her Muslim father abandoned the family. In 2014, a Sudanese court declared her a Muslim—because her father was Muslim—and sentenced her to death for apostasy and to flogging for adultery, because her marriage to a Christian man was deemed void under sharia. She gave birth to her second child while shackled in a Sudanese prison, awaiting execution. International outrage eventually secured her release, and she was granted asylum in the United States. But her case was not exceptional. It was simply visible.

Or consider Raif Badawi, a Saudi blogger who was sentenced to ten years in prison and one thousand lashes—delivered in public, fifty at a time, each Friday—for "insulting Islam" through his writing. His offense was not violent. It was intellectual. He questioned the untouchable, and criticized "the sacred," because he thought differently. Under sharia, that is unacceptable and intolerable.

Closer to home, consider the experience of countless Muslim Americans who have quietly left Islam and now live in fear—not of the government, which cannot touch them, but of their own families and communities. The threats are real. The social violence is real. "Honor" killings and violent attacks on apostates occur in Western countries with Muslim immigrant communities, including the United States. The perpetrators often cite, explicitly, the Islamic law regarding apostasy as their justification. They are not misquoting their tradition. They are applying it.

THE AMERICAN CONVERT'S SECRET

Spend any time in communities of former Muslims in the United States—and they exist, in significant and growing numbers, organized in groups like Ex-Muslims of North America—and you will hear the same story told in a thousand different voices.

A young woman raised in a devout Muslim household in Michigan begins to doubt her faith in college. She reads the Quran, she questions Muhammad's actions, she eventually concludes that she no longer believes. For years she practices what former Muslims call "stealth apostasy"—attending Friday prayers, observing Ramadan publicly, performing all the outward rituals—because she knows that if her family discovers her true beliefs, the consequences will be severe. She is not afraid of legal consequences—she is in America—but of social, familial, and potentially physical consequences that the law of apostasy, transmitted through her community's culture, has made entirely credible. "If my father found out," one such woman wrote in an online forum, "he would not call the police. He would handle it himself. That is what Islam teaches him to do."

Browse any online discussion forum where former Muslims share their experiences and you will find this dynamic described with heartbreaking consistency. The fear is not theoretical. The theological justification for the fear is not invented. It comes directly from the hadith that has governed Islamic communities for fourteen centuries: whoever changes his Islamic religion, kill him.

What makes this threat particularly relevant to the American constitutional question is not just that individual families act on this principle. It is that Islamist organizations operating in the United States are actively working to ensure that this principle is never challenged, never criticized, and never clearly named. Apostasy laws are consistently defended in Islamist advocacy as a “religious matter”—something that Western observers have no standing to evaluate or condemn. The freedom to criticize those laws, to name them for what they are, is itself framed as an attack on Islam. Buzzwords like ‘bigotry’ and ‘Islamophobia’ are ready to be weaponized. We will return to that argument in Chapter Three.

WHAT THE FIRST AMENDMENT GUARANTEES

The First Amendment’s Free Exercise Clause was written to make this kind of coercion impossible in America. Its premise is simple and revolutionary: every human being possesses a right to follow his own conscience before God—or before no God at all—without interference from the state, so long as his following does not infringe anyone else’s similar rights. The government cannot compel religious belief. It cannot punish religious disbelief. It cannot penalize the decision to change faiths, abandon faith, or embrace a faith that the majority despises.

This principle was not an accident of drafting. It was the hard-won product of bitter experience. Roger Williams, banished from Massachusetts Bay Colony for his religious views, believed that state-coerced religion was a sin against both God and humanity. John Leland, the Baptist minister who pressed James Madison to include religious liberty in the Bill of Rights, argued that the moment government begins to define what you must believe, it has become a tyrant over the soul. Thomas Jefferson, writing the Virginia Statute for Religious Freedom in 1786, declared that God himself had made the mind free—and that any attempt by earthly authority to coerce it was a departure from the divine plan.

The Constitution these men crafted reflects that conviction completely.

In America, you may leave any religion—including Islam—without legal consequence. Period. No asterisk. No exception.

Classical sharia does not offer an asterisk either. Its exception runs in the opposite direction. Leaving Islam is not a protected right. It is a capital crime. You can accept Islam, but you can never abandon it. The Muslim who walks away from Islam does not merely lose standing in his community. He forfeits, under the sharia as explained in every major school of Islamic jurisprudence, the very right to live.

These two positions cannot be reconciled. They are diametrically opposed answers to the most fundamental question in the relationship between the individual and the law: does a human being own his conscience?

America's answer is yes—the individual owns his conscience, completely and inviolably.

Sharia's answer, in its authoritative form, is no—and the penalty for acting otherwise can be death.

THE DEFENSE YOU WILL HEAR—AND WHY IT FAILS

When confronted with apostasy law, defenders of sharia in Western contexts typically offer one of three responses. Each deserves a direct answer.

The first response is that apostasy laws applied only to traitors—that in early Islam, leaving the faith was always combined with political rebellion, and the death penalty was for the treason, not the theology. This argument has a superficial appeal but collapses under examination. The hadith recorded in *Sahih al-Bukhari* does not say "whoever leaves Islam and takes up arms against Muslims." It says "whoever changes his Islamic religion." The classical jurists—who were careful scholars, not careless readers—understood this hadith to apply to the act of apostasy itself, regardless of whether it was accompanied by political rebellion. Ibn Qudama, al-Nawawi, Ibn Taymiyya—none of them limited the ruling to armed traitors. They applied it to anyone who abandoned Islam.

The second response is that "nobody really enforces apostasy laws anymore"—that modernity has effectively retired the penalty, even in Muslim-majority countries. Tell that to Meriam Ibrahim, shackled in a Sudanese prison in 2014. Tell that to the tens of thousands of people living under sharia-governed legal systems in Saudi Arabia, Iran, Afghanistan, and elsewhere, for whom apostasy remains a capital crime in active law. Tell that to the former Muslims living in Western countries whose families have threatened them with violence in direct reference to Islamic teaching on apostasy.

The third response—the most politically sophisticated—is that sharia's apostasy laws are merely a private religious matter, protected by the First Amendment's Free Exercise Clause, and that calling them out is an act of bigotry and 'Islamophobia.' This argument might be the most dangerous of the three, because it attempts to use America's commitment to religious freedom as a shield for a doctrine that destroys religious freedom. This ploy is textbook within Islamism. The Free Exercise Clause protects religious belief and personal practice. It does not protect enforcement of the death penalty against people who change their beliefs. Labeling a death sentence a "religious matter" does not bring it within the protection of the First Amendment. It simply dresses a human rights atrocity in religious language in hopes that Americans will be too naïve and polite to look beneath the robe.

WHY IT MATTERS IN AMERICA

Some readers may be thinking: this penalty for apostasy is terrible, but it happens over there—in Saudi Arabia, in Iran, in Afghanistan. It doesn't happen here. American law would never permit it. Why devote a chapter of a book to a problem that our Constitution has already solved? The answer is that the Constitution solves the problem only as long as Americans understand what the Constitution is defending against—and insist that it be defended.

Islamist organizations in the United States do not *currently* have the political power to implement apostasy law. But their strategic goal—as documented in their own writings expressed in their own theological frameworks—is to expand sharia-compatible norms in American law and culture incrementally, over the long term, using every tool that American democracy provides. Part of that project involves making apostasy law off limits to open discussion—treating it as a protected religious belief that cannot be named, criticized, or legally addressed lest the critic be accused of bigotry. Islamists exploit, abuse, and misuse our laws and liberties to destroy our freedoms.

When a society loses the capacity to name a venom, it loses the ability to defend itself against it. The First Amendment protects the right to change your religion. Protecting that right requires being willing to say clearly that any legal system which punishes that change with death is incompatible with the Constitution—not in one interpretation, not in some historical application, but in its classical, authoritative, fully-documented form.

The freedom to apostatize is one of the most basic freedoms a human being can possess. It is freedom of thought made concrete—the right to follow your mind and your conscience wherever they lead, without fear of the state. America was built on that freedom. Sharia, as documented and practiced, was built to extinguish it.

That conflict is alive, active, and taking place right now—in courtrooms, in communities, in the private calculations of men and women across this country who know, from experience, that in some communities the hadith still carries more weight than the Constitution.

It is time Americans knew exactly what that hadith says.

3

YOU CAN SAY ANYTHING—EXCEPT THAT—WHY SHARIA'S BLASPHEMY LAWS ARE THE FIRST AMENDMENT'S WORST ENEMY

In 1977, a group of American Nazis applied for a permit to march through Skokie, Illinois—a suburb of Chicago where thousands of Holocaust survivors lived. The residents were understandably horrified. Their pain was genuine and profound. The march was designed specifically to wound them. And the Supreme Court of the United States ruled that it could proceed.

The case became one of the most cited illustrations of what the First Amendment means in practice. It does not protect only comfortable speech. It does not protect only speech that the majority approves of, or speech that causes no offense, or speech that powerful institutions find acceptable. It protects speech that is ugly, wrong, hurtful, and deliberately provocative—because the moment you grant the government the power to silence speech it finds offensive, you have handed the government a weapon that will always, eventually, be turned against you.

That principle is the beating heart of American democracy. It is also the principle that sharia's blasphemy laws are designed to suppress and annihilate.

Under sharia, criticizing Muhammad is a capital crime, punishable by death. Not in one school of jurisprudence, nor only in one historical period. In the mainstream, classical, authoritative tradition of Islamic law, speaking against Muhammad, mocking the Quran, or insulting any Islamic sacred item is an offense for which the prescribed penalty is execution. And unlike apostasy, where some schools of jurisprudence allow the offender to recant and be spared, the dominant classical opinion on blasphemy holds that repentance does not save you. The insult, once uttered, has already earned its penalty.

This chapter is about where that doctrine came from, what it has done to real human beings, and why it cannot coexist with the First Amendment.

THE MAN WHO WROTE A POEM—AND PAID WITH HIS LIFE

To understand sharia's blasphemy doctrine, you need to understand where it was born—not in the writings of medieval Muslim thinkers, but in the personal decisions of Muhammad himself.

Ka'b ibn al-Ashraf was a Jewish poet living in Medina at the time of Muhammad. After the Battle of Badr in 624 AD, in which the early Muslim community defeated a much larger Meccan force, Ka'b traveled to Mecca and composed elegies mourning the Meccan dead—poetry that was *perceived* as hostile to Muhammad and to Islam itself. He was a critic, a man who used words as weapons in the political conflicts of his day.

Muhammad's response was to ask, in front of his companions: "Who will deal with Ka'b ibn al-Ashraf? He has hurt Allah and His Messenger." A companion named Ibn Maslama volunteered. Muhammad gave his personal permission—recorded in *Sahih al-Bukhari* and *Sahih Muslim*, the two most authoritative hadith collections in Sunni Islam—for the mission. Ibn Maslama and a small group of men gained Ka'b's trust through deception, lured him out of his home at night, and killed him. To show their devotion and dedication to Muhammad, they brought his head to Islam's prophet.

When the other Jews of Medina were terrified by the assassination and came to Muhammad to protest, his response—recorded in the hadith—was to tell them that the killing of Ka'b was justified by his offense against Allah and his Messenger. The message was clear and intentional: those who insult Muhammad do so at the cost of their lives.

Ka'b ibn al-Ashraf was not the only one. The historical record of early Islam documents a pattern of people being killed on Muhammad's explicit order or with his explicit approval for the offense of mocking or criticizing him.

Asma bint Marwan was a poetess who composed verses condemning Muhammad and calling her tribe to resist him. She was killed in her home at night, reportedly while she was nursing her infant child, by a man who had received Muhammad's blessing for the act. When the killer reported what he had done, Muhammad's response was that not even two goats would butt their heads over her killing—meaning her life was of no consequence given her offense.

Abu ʿAfak was an elderly Jewish man, reportedly over one hundred years old, who composed satirical verses mocking Muhammad's killings and his growing political power. He was assassinated in his sleep. Muhammad reportedly asked who would deal with this man, and a companion carried out the killing.

Abdullah ibn Khatal was killed on the day of the conquest of Mecca—one of the few individuals whom Muhammad specifically ordered to be executed even inside the sacred precincts of the Kaaba, where killing was traditionally forbidden. His offense included, among other things, having composed songs that mocked Muhammad, which were performed by two slave girls. Both slave girls were also ordered to be killed; one was captured and executed, the other escaped and was later pardoned.

These are not isolated stories dug up by hostile critics. They are narrated in the foundational Islamic sources—the *sira*, the biographical literature of Muhammad's life, and the hadith collections—as Islamic examples of appropriate, even praiseworthy responses to the offense of insulting God's messenger. They became the legal precedents on which a thousand years of Islamic blasphemy jurisprudence was built.

WHAT THE JURISTS BUILT

Islamic legal scholars systematized these stories into a comprehensive legal doctrine—one of the most detailed and lethal in the history of religious law.

Ibn Taymiyya, the fourteenth-century Hanbali jurist whose writings continue to influence Islamist movements worldwide, devoted an entire book to the subject— *Al-Sarim al-Maslul ala Shatim al-Rasul*, which translates as "The Drawn Sword Against the One Who Insults the Messenger." Ibn Taymiyya's argument, developed with meticulous legal reasoning across hundreds of pages, is that killing the person who insults Muhammad is not merely permissible—it is obligatory. The sword is already drawn. It does not need to wait for a court's permission. Importantly, Ibn Taymiyya wrote this book in 1293–1294, in direct response to a specific incident involving a Christian monk who had insulted Muhammad.

Ibn Taymiyya's argument rested on several pillars. First, Muhammad established the precedent through his actions—and whatever Muhammad did is, by definition, the correct Islamic response. Second, the insult to Muhammad is not merely a personal offense; it is an attack on the foundations of Islam itself—because Muhammad is the channel through which divine revelation reached humanity. To attack Muhammad, says Ibn Taymiyya, is to attack the Quran. To attack the Quran is to attack Allah. The offense, therefore, cannot be viewed as a private matter with a civil remedy. It demands the ultimate penalty. Third—and this is the point that distinguishes Islamic blasphemy law most sharply from every other legal tradition—Ibn Taymiyya argued that repentance does not expunge the penalty. A person who insults Muhammad and then claims to repent is still to be killed, because the crime against the community and against Allah's honor has already been committed. Remorse does not undo it.

Ibn Qayyim al-Jawziyya, Ibn Taymiyya's most distinguished student and intellectual heir, extended this analysis in his own writings, cataloguing the cases from the prophetic period and systematizing the legal ruling of death for the one who insults Muhammad, with no exception for repentance, and no distinction between Muslims and non-Muslims as offenders. A Christian who criticizes Muhammad in a Muslim-governed society is as liable as a Muslim who does the same. The protection of Muhammad's honor is not an internal Islamic matter. It is a universal legal obligation—universal, that is, within the world that sharia governs.

These are not obscure scholars. Ibn Taymiyya and Ibn Qayyim are among the most widely read, most frequently cited, and most institutionally influential jurists in the history of Islamic law. Their books are taught in Islamic universities. Their rulings are referenced in contemporary fatwas. Their arguments underlie blasphemy laws in Pakistan, Saudi Arabia, Iran, and elsewhere. When Pakistani clerics call for the execution of a Christian woman accused of insulting Muhammad, they are citing a jurisprudential tradition that stretches in an unbroken line from Muhammad's own commands.

PAKISTAN: WHERE THE LAW KILLS WOMEN

No nation in the world has made sharia's blasphemy doctrine more ruthlessly concrete than Pakistan—and no modern nation offers a more instructive case study in what that doctrine actually looks like when it has the force of law.

Pakistan's blasphemy statutes, codified under Section 295-C of the Pakistan Penal Code, prescribe the death penalty for "defiling the name of the Prophet Muhammad." The law requires no proof of intent. It requires no evidence that the accused intended to insult Islam's prophet. An accusation is enough to trigger arrest, imprisonment, and trial—and, frequently, mob violence long before any court reaches a verdict. Section 295-C has been applied in Pakistan overwhelmingly against religious minorities—Christians and Hindus—but also against Muslims who were deemed insufficiently reverent.

The case of Asia Bibi became known around the world, and it deserves to be told here in full.

Asia Bibi was a Christian farmworker in Punjab province. In 2009, she was picking berries with a group of Muslim women when a dispute broke out over a bowl of water. Asia Bibi had drunk from it; the Muslim women refused to drink after her, on the grounds that she was a Christian and therefore religiously unclean. An argument followed. A few days later, Asia Bibi was accused of having insulted Muhammad during the argument. She denied it. It did not matter. She was arrested, tried under Section 295-C, convicted, and sentenced to death. She spent more than eight years on death row, much of it in solitary confinement, before Pakistan's Supreme Court—under extraordinary international pressure and amid violent protests from Muslim groups demanding her execution—finally acquitted her in 2018.

Asia could not remain in Pakistan after her acquittal. The threats against her life were too credible. She and her family were granted asylum in Canada. The judge who wrote her acquittal received death threats. Two politicians who had publicly called for her release—Punjab Governor Salman Taseer and Minorities Minister Shahbaz Bhatti—were assassinated. Taseer was shot twenty-seven times by his own bodyguard, who later said he acted to defend the honor of Muhammad. The bodyguard was celebrated in parts of Pakistan as a hero. Lawyers who volunteered to defend Asia Bibi were forced by death threats to abandon her case.

While Asia Bibi's story is extreme in its duration and international visibility, it is not extreme in its basic structure. Since Pakistan's blasphemy laws were strengthened in the 1980s under General Zia ul-Haq, hundreds of people have been accused, imprisoned, and in many cases killed—often by mob violence before any legal proceeding—for the offense of saying something someone claimed insulted Muhammad. The accused tend to be poor, uneducated, and from religious minorities. Their accusers frequently have personal grudges, property disputes, or political axes to grind. The charge of blasphemy is a weapon of choice precisely because it is lethal and so immune to rebuttal: once the accusation is made, even defending oneself can be portrayed as a further insult.

Pakistan is not an outlier. It is an example of what sharia's blasphemy doctrine looks like when it is given institutional power.

CHARLIE HEBDO, SALMAN RUSHDIE, AND THE LONG ARM OF ISLAMIC BLASPHEMY LAW

Islam's prohibition of insult does not stay within the borders of Muslim-majority countries. It travels.

In 1989, the Ayatollah Khomeini of Iran issued a fatwa—a formal religious ruling—calling for the death of Salman Rushdie, a British novelist who was widely portrayed as an ex-Muslim, for his book *The Satanic Verses*—which Khomeini declared blasphemous against Islam. Rushdie had never set foot in Iran. He was a British citizen living in London. None of that mattered. Khomeini's fatwa declared it the duty of every Muslim to kill him if given the opportunity. He placed a bounty that eventually reaching millions of dollars on Rushdie's life. Rushdie spent decades in hiding under British government protection. The book's Japanese translator was stabbed to death. Its Italian translator was stabbed and seriously wounded. Its Norwegian publisher was shot. In 2022—thirty-three years after the fatwa was issued, long after Rushdie had emerged from hiding and resumed public life—a Muslim man, American-born of Lebanese parentage, attacked him on a lecture stage in New York, stabbing him multiple times and leaving him permanently blind in one eye. The perpetrator was a young American man whose motivations, by his own account, were directly founded upon the Islamic doctrine that insulting Muhammad demands lethal retribution.

In January 2015, two gunmen entered the Paris offices of the satirical magazine *Charlie Hebdo* and opened fire, killing twelve people. Their stated reason was that the magazine had published cartoons depicting Muhammad. Before they fled the scene, one of the gunmen shouted, in Arabic, "We have avenged the Prophet." These acts of violence were explicitly framed and clearly executed by their perpetrators as the enforcement of Islamic blasphemy law on Western soil—the fulfillment of the doctrine that Ibn Taymiyya articulated and that Muhammad modeled when he asked, "who will deal with Ka'b ibn al-Ashraf?"

In 2005, a Danish newspaper published cartoons of Muhammad. Responses across the Muslim world included mass protests, the burning of Danish embassies, and the deaths of more than two hundred people in riot-related violence. Several of the Charlie Hebdo cartoonists required round-the-clock police protection for years. One cartoonist, Kurt Westergaard, survived an axe attack in his home by a Somali man who had come to kill him in defense of Muhammad's honor.

In 2020, a French middle school teacher named Samuel Paty was beheaded by an eighteen-year-old Chechen immigrant in the street outside his school after showing his students cartoons of Muhammad as part of a lesson on freedom of expression. French President Emmanuel Macron called the beheading an Islamist terrorist attack. Immediately afterward, Islamist voices in multiple countries called for boycotts of French products, and several politicians in Muslim-majority countries praised the killing, directly or implicitly. The Organization of Islamic Cooperation (OIC) issued statements criticizing France for its defense of the cartoons rather than condemning the murder.

These incidents are not isolated occurrences connected only by a common religion. They are connected by a common legal doctrine—the idea that insulting Muhammad is a capital offense and that any Muslim who carries out the sentence is performing a righteous act pleasing to Allah and honoring Muhammad. That doctrine comes directly from Muhammad's own precedents, was systematized by Islamic jurists, and is applied today formally in courtrooms and on street corners by vigilantes who are then excused or even praised by the authorities.

THE ONLINE WORLD: BLASPHEMY IN REAL TIME

You do not need to look only at courtrooms and assassinations to see how sharia's blasphemy doctrine operates. You can find it in any comment section, any social media thread, any online forum where someone dares to criticize Muhammad or the Quran.

Post a critical question about Muhammad on virtually any Islamic discussion platform and watch what happens. Within minutes—sometimes seconds—the responses will include demands that you retract your statement, accusations that you have committed an unforgivable offense, and frequently open statements that your life is forfeit. "You deserve to die." "In a real Islamic state you would be executed." "May Allah punish you for this." These are not expressions of hurt feelings. They are statements of legal principle—the principle that the honor of Muhammad is protected by a law that prescribes death for its violation, and that the only question is who will carry out the sentence.

Former Muslims who have spoken publicly about leaving Islam often describe receiving death threats specifically framed in terms of blasphemy. They did not merely leave the faith—they spoke about why. That speech, in the eyes of those who threaten them, triggered the blasphemy provision alongside the apostasy provision. The combination is lethal in both directions.

WHAT THE FIRST AMENDMENT WAS BUILT FOR

Popular speech needs no protection. The crowd already defends it. James Madison wrote the First Amendment precisely to protect unpopular speech—speech that offends, speech that challenges, speech that powerful institutions want silenced.

The U.S. Supreme Court has consistently affirmed this point for decades. In *Matal v. Tam* (2017), the Court unanimously struck down a law that prohibited the registration of "disparaging" trademarks, with Justice Samuel Alito writing that "the proudest boast of our free speech jurisprudence is that we protect the freedom to express the thought that we hate." In *Snyder v. Phelps* (2011), the Court upheld the right of the Westboro Baptist Church to picket military funerals with signs reading "God Hates Fags." In *Texas v. Johnson* (1989), the Court upheld the right to burn the American flag. The foundational principle is clear: American government can neither designate certain ideas as too offensive to express, nor use the law to punish those who express them.

This principle means, specifically, that under the First Amendment, you have an absolute constitutional right to criticize Muhammad. You have the right to draw cartoons of him. You have the right to write books questioning his prophethood, his moral character, his military campaigns, or his marriages. You have the right to say, in print or in public, that you find Islamic doctrines repugnant, and that, since Muhammad married a six-years-old girl, he was a pedophile. These are protected expressions, not crimes—not because the Constitution is hostile to Islam, but because the Constitution treats every religion equally, which means no religion gets a special exemption from criticism, mockery, or rejection.

Sharia does not offer such equality. Rather, it carves out a specific zone of tolerated speech—that which does not dishonor Muhammad—and prescribes death for anyone who violates it. That zone has no parallel in any other legal system that the modern world would recognize as compatible with human rights. It is more than a mere different approach to speech regulation. It is the categorical rejection of the principle on which the First Amendment rests: that the government cannot silence ideas.

And unlike apostasy law, where the threat is directed at those who change their religion, blasphemy law reaches outward. It reaches non-Muslims. It reaches secular citizens who never signed up for any religious code. It reaches Danish cartoonists, French schoolteachers, British novelists, and American bloggers. It claims jurisdiction over anyone who speaks—anywhere, in any language, in any country—in a way that someone decides has offended the honor of a seventh-century Arabian prophet.

Sharia's prescribed penalty in this matter is, in other words, an attempt at universal censorship enforced by the threat of death.

THE DEFENSE YOU WILL HEAR—AND WHY IT FAILS

Defenders of sharia's blasphemy doctrine in Western contexts typically make two arguments.

The first is that blasphemy laws are not uniquely Islamic—that Western countries have had blasphemy laws too, and that therefore singling out sharia's version is selective and unfair. This argument is historically true in a narrow sense, but also deeply misleading. Yes, English common law classified blasphemy as an offense until it was abolished in 2008. Yes, several European countries have hate speech laws, and yes, these at times have been applied to religious criticism. But there is a categorical difference between a civil penalty for religious offense in a modern democratic state—subject to legislative repeal, judicial review, and human rights protections—and a divinely mandated death sentence that Islamic jurists explicitly say cannot be reduced, negotiated, or reformed because it comes from Allah himself. The English blasphemy law had not resulted in a single execution in over two centuries before it was abolished. By contrast, although Pakistan has never executed anyone under Section 295-C, the law has produced dozens of death sentences, hundreds of people on death row, nearly a hundred vigilante killings since 1990, and the assassination of the governor who called for its reform—enforced not by the state's hand but by a society the law has licensed to kill. So, the comparison is not serious.

A second objection is that violent responses to blasphemy are the work of "radicals" who have distorted true Islamic teaching, and that mainstream Islam condemns them. This argument requires ignoring the fact that the men who killed Ka'b ibn al-Ashraf, Asma bint Marwan, and Abu ʿAfak were acting on Muhammad's explicit instructions. It requires ignoring Ibn Taymiyya's book-length legal argument that killing the blasphemer is obligatory and divinely mandated. It requires ignoring that Pakistan's blasphemy law is the creation of a state that explicitly grounds its legal code in classical sharia. It requires ignoring that virtually every major Sunni institution—including Al-Azhar University in Egypt, the most prestigious institution of Sunni Islamic scholarship in the world—has historically upheld the death penalty for blasphemy as classical Islamic law, even when individual scholars have called for its reform.

The severe violence is not a distortion of the doctrine. The violence is the "sacred" doctrine, applied.

WHY THIS MATTERS IN AMERICA

The United States do not have blasphemy laws. They *cannot* have them—the First Amendment forbids it. But sharia's blasphemy doctrine is already operating in America in subtler ways—through social pressure, through intimidation, through a systematic effort to make certain ideas unspeakable.

When a university cancels a lecture by a critic of Islam under pressure from student groups citing 'Islamophobia.'[1] When a newspaper declines to republish the Charlie Hebdo cartoons while it would readily publish similar images mocking Christianity or Judaism.[2] When a politician refuses to use the words "Islamic" and "terrorism" in the same sentence.[3] When a publisher drops a book critical of Muhammad because of threats. When a teacher thinks twice before assigning a text that includes even a sympathetic discussion of Muhammad's more controversial actions. These are not formal applications of blasphemy law. But they are its cultural shadow—the chilling effect that sharia's blasphemy doctrine casts over free societies when the threat of violence is credible enough to modify behavior without any formal law being passed.

Samuel Paty did not live in a country in which blasphemy was outlawed. He was murdered anyway.

The First Amendment does not merely permit criticism of Islam. It demands that such criticism be protected as vigorously, as unconditionally, and as defiantly as any other form of protected speech. Not because Islam deserves special hostility, but because the moment any religion succeeds in placing itself above criticism in a free society—through law, or through violence, or through the fear that makes people self-censor without being told to—that society has ceased to be free in the most fundamental sense.

The American Founders understood this fact. The line they drew in the First Amendment was not designed to single out any religion. It was drawn against the principle—present in every religious legal system that has ever sought political power—that some ideas are too sacred to question and some men are too holy to criticize.

Muhammad ordered the killing of a poet for his words. His jurists built a legal system around that precedent. That system is now operating in Muslim courtrooms and on sidewalks, throughout cities and towns, on social media platforms and in university seminar rooms, pressing against the wall that the First Amendment erected. That wall must hold.

---

1. In April 2014, Brandeis University rescinded its invitation to Ayaan Hirsi Ali to receive an honorary degree at its commencement, after protests by students, faculty, and outside organizations accused her of Islamophobia. See Ayaan Hirsi Ali, "Here's What I Would Have Said at Brandeis," Wall Street Journal, April 10, 2014.

2. Rem Rieder, "The Missing Charlie Hebdo Cartoons," *Columbia Journalism Review*, January 8, 2015.

3. "President Barack Obama: Why I Won't Say 'Islamic Terrorism,'" CNN, September 28, 2016.

4

SOME ARE MORE EQUAL THAN OTHERS —HOW SHARIA'S LEGAL HIERARCHY OF HUMAN WORTH VIOLATES THE FOURTEENTH AMENDMENT

There is a sentence in the Fourteenth Amendment to the United States Constitution that is as simple and as radical as any sentence in the history of human governance: No state shall deny to any person within its jurisdiction the equal protection of the laws. Eleven words. No asterisks. No exceptions for religion, race, gender, or national origin. Every person—not every citizen, not every believer, not every man—every person stands equal before the law.

That sentence was written in blood. That is to say, it was ratified in 1868, three years after the Civil War ended, specifically to dismantle a legal system that had assigned human beings different legal rights based on what they were rather than what they had done. The men who wrote it understood, from a brutal national experience, what happens when a society encodes hierarchy into its law—when the legal system itself declares that some lives are worth more than others, that some voices carry more weight in court, that some people owe duties to others who owe them nothing in return.

Classical sharia is such a system. It does not merely tolerate inequality as an imperfection or a historical accident. It mandates it as divine will. It builds hierarchy into its foundations—hierarchy based on religion, hierarchy based on gender—and it does so with the full weight of Quranic authority and prophetic command.

This chapter is about what that hierarchy looks like in practice, why it exists in sharia's own terms, and why it cannot coexist with the Fourteenth Amendment.

WOMEN FIRST: THE FOUNDATION OF SHARIA'S HIERARCHY

Before we consider the treatment of Christians and Jews under Islamic law, we must reckon with an even more foundational inequality—one that affects half of the human race and that sharia does not merely permit but commands. The subordination of women in classical sharia is doctrinal, grounded in the very words of Muhammad.

In a hadith recorded in *Sahih al-Bukhari*—the same authoritative collection cited throughout this book—Muhammad stated his view on the nature of women with disarming directness. When a group of women came to offer charitable donations after a sermon, Muhammad said to them: "O women, give charity, for I have seen that you form the majority of the dwellers of Hell." The women asked why. Muhammad explained: "You curse frequently and are ungrateful to your husbands. I have not seen anyone more deficient in intelligence and religion than you."

A woman in the crowd asked what deficiency in intelligence and religion meant. Muhammad answered: "Is not the testimony of two women equal to the testimony of one man?" When she agreed, he said: "This is the deficiency in her intelligence. And is it not the case that a woman does not pray and does not fast during her menses?" When she agreed, he said: "This is the deficiency in her religion."

This hadith is *sahih*—meaning sound, authoritative, and authenticated—and it has been cited by Islamic jurists across every major school of jurisprudence for over a thousand years to justify specific, concrete legal inferiorities and disabilities imposed on women. Muhammad embedded his view of women's nature directly into the structure of Islamic law.

Concerning political leadership, Muhammad was similarly strident. When news reached him that the Persians had made a woman their ruler, he declared: "A people who place a woman in charge of their affairs will never succeed." This hadith, also in *Sahih al-Bukhari*, became the classical Islamic basis for sharia's prohibition on women holding positions of political authority over men—a prohibition that is not merely a conservative cultural tendency but actually a legal ruling based upon Muhammad's authority.

The Quran reinforces these positions with its own explicit hierarchy. Surah 4:34 states: "Men are in charge of women, because Allah has given the one more than the other, and because they support them from their means." The verse then instructs that a husband may beat a disobedient wife—but only as a last resort. This passage is not understood by any mainstream Islamic jurist to be merely metaphorical. The jurists have debated the conditions and manner of its application for centuries—but they have not, in the classical tradition, disputed that it establishes male authority as divinely ordained, up to and including physical beating of the wife.

In inheritance law, the Quran is specific: "Allah commands you regarding your children: the share of the male shall be twice that of the female" (Surah 4:11). A daughter inherits half of what a son inherits. A wife inherits one-eighth of her husband's estate if there are children; a husband inherits one-quarter of his wife's estate under the same conditions. The asymmetry runs through the entire inheritance structure of classical sharia, and it is not a human legal choice that can be reformed by legislators. It is a Quranic command.

In court testimony, Muhammad's statement that two women's testimony equals one man's is enforceable law. The classical Maliki, Hanbali, and Shafi'i schools hold that women's testimony is inadmissible in cases involving the *hudud* penalties—the most severe criminal punishments. In financial matters, a rule of two women per one man applies. The Hanafi school is somewhat more permissive on civil matters, but the fundamental principle—that a woman's word carries less legal weight than a man's—pervades classical Islamic jurisprudence as a structural feature, not an anomaly.

I sincerely encourage American woman reading the above to pause and let it land. Under classical sharia, her word in a court of law is worth half of any man's. Her inheritance from her father will be, by law and not subject to the preference of father or any other person, half that of her brother. Her husband has Quranic authority over her conduct and, in classical jurisprudence, the right to physical discipline. She may not, by Muhammad's command, lead a nation. That said, some Muslim-majority countries have elected or appointed women as prime ministers or heads of government in recent decades. However, these cases do not reflect the application of classical sharia; rather, they occur in secular or hybrid systems that have set aside or heavily modified traditional Islamic legal rulings on female leadership. These are legal rulings grounded in the Quran and the sahih hadith—the same sources that Islamist movements cite as the authoritative basis for Islamic governance.

THE DHIMMI SYSTEM: A LEGAL ARCHITECTURE OF INFERIORITY

If the treatment of women represents sharia's *internal* hierarchy—the inequality it imposes within the Muslim community—its treatment of non-Muslims, particularly Christians and Jews, represents its *external* hierarchy: the legal order it imposes on those outside the faith.

The Arabic word *dhimmi* comes from the root meaning "obligation" or "guarantee." In classical Islamic jurisprudence, *dhimma* is a stigma that refers to the status of non-Muslims—specifically Jews and Christians, designated in the Quran as "People of the Book"—living under Islamic governance. These people are given a conditional "protection"—meaning the Islamic state will not kill them as it would polytheists—but that protection comes at a severe and degrading price, and it is shot through with legal inequalities completely inconsistent with the Fourteenth Amendment.

The Quranic foundation for the dhimma system is explicitly stated in Surah 9:29: "Fight those who do not believe in Allah or in the Last Day and who do not consider unlawful what Allah and his Messenger have made unlawful and who do not abide by the religion of truth from those who were given the Scripture—until they give the *jizya* willingly while they are humbled."

Read that verse carefully. The word translated as "humbled" in many English versions is, in the Arabic original, *saghirun*—subdued, humiliated, lowered, made small. The classical commentators of the Quran are unanimous that this humiliation is not incidental to the *jizya* payment. Rather, it is the point. The renowned Quranic commentator Ibn Kathir—whose *tafsir*, or Quranic commentary, is among the most widely read in the Islamic world—explained that the *jizya* must be paid by the dhimmi while he is standing and the Muslim tax collector is seated, that the dhimmi must be struck on the neck or the cheek as the payment is made, and that he must feel himself "disgraced and humiliated." Ibn Kathir was not inventing this interpretation. He was recording the consensus of classical Islamic scholarship on what Surah 9:29 requires.

This word is the one that describes Christians and Jews under classical sharia: subdued. Not valued as equal, not even tolerated as equals who happen to pay a different tax. Subdued—legally, ceremonially, institutionally—as a permanent reminder of Islam's supremacy and their own second-class status.

The word dhimmi itself has become, in the communities where this system was applied, a term of religious and social stigma—a word you called someone to mark them as lesser, as permanently subordinate, as outside the circle of full human dignity that Islamic society reserved for its Muslim members. No American of any faith should be comfortable with a legal system that assigns that label to their fellow citizens—and yet that is precisely the system that classical sharia mandates.

BLOOD MONEY: WHAT YOUR LIFE IS WORTH UNDER SHARIA

Perhaps the most viscerally revealing illustration of sharia's legal hierarchy is the doctrine of *diya*—blood money, the compensation paid for killing or injuring another person.

In classical Islamic jurisprudence, diya is not merely a civil remedy. It is a precise legal valuation of human life—and that valuation varies explicitly based on who the victim is.

The full diya for a Muslim man is established by hadith at one hundred camels, or its monetary equivalent—a substantial sum that represented the full legal value of any Muslim male's life. The diya for a Muslim woman, in the majority classical opinion, is half that—fifty camels. The diya for a Christian or Jewish victim—a dhimmi—is explicitly set at half the diya of a Muslim victim in the Maliki, Hanbali, and Shafiʿi schools. The Hanafi school sets it at the same amount as for a Muslim, making it the most generous of the four schools on this point—but still maintains other inequalities that compromise that nominal equality in practice.

Think about what this difference means in concrete terms. Under classical sharia, if a Muslim man kills a Christian man, the financial penalty is half what it would be if he had killed a Muslim. The life of the Christian, in the explicit legal calculus of Islamic jurisprudence, is worth fifty percent of the life of the Muslim. This valuation is written law—derived from the hadith, elaborated by the jurists, and applied in sharia courts for over a thousand years.

The Fourteenth Amendment's equal protection guarantee rests on precisely the opposite premise: that *every* person's life, safety, and dignity are equally protected by the law, regardless of religion, regardless of race, regardless of anything. There is no half-price version of equal protection. There is no discount diya in the American constitutional tradition. The moment a legal system assigns different legal values to different lives based on the religion of the victim, it has violated equal protection as thoroughly as it is possible to violate it.

THE COURTROOM: WHERE INEQUALITY BECOMES SYSTEMIC

The diya disparity is only one dimension of the legal inequality that classical sharia builds into its treatment of non-Muslims. The courtroom is where that inequality becomes most systematically oppressive.

In classical sharia, the testimony of a non-Muslim against a Muslim is either inadmissible or severely discounted. The Maliki, Hanbali, and Shafiʾi schools hold, with varying degrees of specificity, that a Christian or Jew cannot testify against a Muslim in most categories of legal dispute. The Hanafi school permits non-Muslim testimony in civil matters but maintains restrictions in criminal cases involving hudud punishments. Across all four schools, the principle is the same: in a legal system governed by sharia, a Muslim's word outweighs a non-Muslim's word as a matter of constitutional structure, not mere judicial discretion.

The practical implication is staggering. A Christian who is wronged by a Muslim—robbed, assaulted, defrauded—and who brings his complaint to a sharia court, may find that his own testimony is inadmissible or that the Muslim defendant's denial, supported by the testimony of Muslim witnesses, automatically prevails. He has no legal recourse not because his case lacks merit, but because the legal system has categorically disqualified his voice because he is non-Muslim.

This disparity is not ancient history. In Egypt, in Saudi Arabia, in

Pakistan, in Iran, in every country that applies classical sharia as its governing law, Christian and Jewish citizens navigate a legal system that treats their testimony as worth less than that of their Muslim neighbors. Christian minorities in Egypt have documented for generations the difficulty of obtaining justice in courts when their adversary is Muslim. The legal structure of sharia makes their disadvantage not an aberration but a feature.

WHAT YOU CANNOT BUILD, WHERE YOU CANNOT PRAY

The dhimmi system extends far beyond courts and compensation. It reaches into the most basic dimensions of communal religious life—and it does so with a thoroughness that would be immediately recognizable to any American as an establishment of religious supremacy.

Under classical sharia, as codified in the jurisprudence of all four major schools and in practical governance documents like the Pact of Umar—a document attributed to the early Islamic state establishing the terms of Christian and Jewish subordination—dhimmis face a comprehensive set of restrictions on public religious life. They may not build new churches or synagogues in Muslim-governed territories. They may not repair existing ones without permission from Muslim authorities—permission that has historically been granted rarely, slowly, and conditionally. They may not ring church bells publicly. They may not display crosses on the exteriors of their buildings. They may not conduct religious processions in public. They may not raise their voices in prayer in ways that Muslims might hear. They may not proselytize—sharing their faith with Muslims or seeking converts from the Muslim community is forbidden on pain of death.

In contemporary Egypt—which does not formally operate under classical sharia, but whose legal system has been profoundly shaped by it—the construction of Christian churches has required a presidential decree since the nineteenth century. Christians form roughly fifteen percent of Egypt's population, one of the largest Christian communities in the Middle East, and yet building a new church can involve decades of bureaucratic obstruction, political negotiation, and even violence. Coptic Christians have been killed, their churches burned, their communities terrorized—and the Egyptian state's response has ranged from tepid to complicit. The legal structure of the dhimmi system does not require formal sharia courts to cast its shadow. It lives in the cultural and institutional assumptions of societies shaped by centuries of Islamic governance.

In Pakistan, Christian communities regularly face accusations of blasphemy that destroy lives and communities. Churches have been burned by mobs responding to blasphemy accusations. Christians have been killed in their homes. Asia Bibi, whose story was told in the previous chapter, is one documented face inside a system containing countless others whose names never reach Western newspapers.

In Iraq and Syria, the ancient Christian communities that had survived fourteen centuries of Islamic governance—often under severe restrictions but with continuous presence—were effectively destroyed in the chaos following the rise of ISIS. ISIS was not applying a fabricated or deviant version of Islamic law when it gave the Christians of Mosul the choice of conversion, the *jizya*, or the sword. It was applying the classical sharia doctrine of dhimmi status with a literalism that made explicit what the tradition had always contained. The dhimmi population of Iraq, which prior to 2003 numbered in the hundreds of thousands, was reduced to a remnant. Their churches are rubble. Their communities, diaspora—scattered.

JIZYA: A STATEMENT, NOT A TAX

Americans are familiar with the concept of taxation. We debate its levels, its fairness, and its purposes endlessly. But in the American tradition—however contentious tax policy may be—a tax is a levy imposed equally on similarly situated persons for the support of public expenses. Taxation is not a ceremony of submission, nor a ritual enactment of your legal and spiritual inferiority.

The *jizya* is something categorically different from mere taxation.

The Quran, and subsequent classical Islamic jurisprudence make explicit that the *jizya* is not merely for the purpose of raising revenue. Rather, it is a performative act of subordination—a regular, embodied reminder that the dhimmi lives under Islamic supremacy and accepts that dominance as one condition of his continued existence. Ibn Kathir's commentary on Surah 9:29, which we have already examined, makes clear that the manner of payment matters as much as the payment itself: the dhimmi must come in person, must feel his degradation, must experience his lowered status in the act of paying.

The Pact of Umar, the foundational document of classical dhimmi governance, specifies that dhimmis must not ride horses (only donkeys, and these without a saddle), must not build houses taller than those of Muslims, must not dress like Muslims, must wear distinguishing clothing that marks them as non-Muslims, must give up their seats to Muslims in public spaces, and must not hold positions of authority over Muslims in any domain of public life.

Read that list again. Forced distinguishing clothing for religious minorities. Legal prohibition on positions of authority. Restrictions on housing, transportation, and public comportment—all designed to make the subordination of non-Muslims visible, constant, and humiliating.

Americans have a term for a system that requires members of a religious minority to wear identifying marks, that bars them from positions of authority, that assigns them separate and inferior rules in housing, transportation, and public life, and that extracts from them a special payment as a condition of toleration. We do not call it "dhimmi protection." We call it what it is: institutionalized discrimination.

The Fourteenth Amendment was written to prohibit just such systematic legal differentiation. Equal protection of the laws means that the law does not assign different rights, different remedies, and different levels of legal personhood based upon religion. It means that the testimony of a Christian in court is worth exactly as much as the testimony of a Muslim. It means that the life of a Jewish victim is as valued as that of a Muslim victim. It means that the right to build a church is equal to the right to build a mosque. It means that no American may be required to demonstrate submission to any religious authority as a condition of living safely in the country.

Classical sharia violates every one of these principles—by design.

"WE ARE SECOND CLASS HERE"

The human experience of living under the dhimmi system is not abstract. It is documented in the testimonies of Christians and Jews who have lived—and are living—under sharia-influenced governance, and in the memories of communities that survived for centuries under Islamic rule only to be finally destroyed in our own lifetimes.

A Coptic Christian woman from Egypt, speaking to researchers documenting minority rights in the Middle East, described the experience this way: "We do not go to the police when something happens, because the police are for Muslims. We do not go to court when we are cheated, because the judge is for Muslims. We pray in our church with the curtains drawn, because if the sound of our prayer offends a neighbor, we will be accused of something. We live here, but we do not belong here. That is what they want us to feel."

An Iraqi Christian man, interviewed after his family fled Mosul in 2014, said: "ISIS gave us the choice that sharia gives: convert, pay the *jizya*, or leave your home. People say ISIS was extreme. But my grandfather told me that we always lived with this choice. It was just quieter. It was always there."

Browse online forums where Christians and former Muslims from Muslim-majority countries discuss their experiences and you will find similar testimonies in abundance. "I was told my church needed permission to fix its roof and the permission never came." "My father was killed and the killer paid half what he would have paid if my father were Muslim." "I went to court and the judge wouldn't look at me because I was Christian." These accounts do not reflect Western misreadings of Islamic practice. They are the lived experience of people subjected to a system whose legal architecture is designed to produce such outcomes.

THE FOURTEENTH AMENDMENT'S ANSWER

The men who wrote the Fourteenth Amendment were students of history. They had seen what a two-tiered legal system does to the people on the lower tier. They had watched the American nation tear itself apart over the question of whether some human beings could be legally denied the same rights as others. Their answer—Section 1 of the Fourteenth Amendment—was categorical: no state shall deny to any person within its jurisdiction the equal protection of the laws.

No state. Any person.

That word—person—is critical. It does not distinguish between believer and unbeliever, Muslim and Christian, man and woman. It assigns the full protection of the law to every human being within the law's reach, regardless of religion, gender, or status in any community's internal hierarchy.

Classical sharia assigns a different legal value to women than to men—in testimony, in inheritance, in marriage, in political authority. It assigns a different legal value to Christians and Jews than to Muslims—in diya, in court testimony, in the right to build houses of worship, in the capacity to hold a position of public authority. It extracts a humiliation tax from non-Muslims as a performative symbol of their subordination. It bars non-Muslims from legal recourse against Muslim adversaries on terms anywhere approaching equality.

Every one of these features is incompatible with the equal protection clause—not as a matter of interpretation, not as a question of degree, but as a categorical conflict between two irreconcilable visions of the law's purpose and function.

American law says that laws exist to protect every person *equally*, regardless of creed. Classical sharia says law exists to maintain the divinely ordained hierarchy in which Islam and Muslims are supreme—and in which everyone else, from women within the faith to Christians and Jews outside it, occupies a lower rung that the law itself enforces and perpetuates.

That is a difference of kind. And it is why the Fourteenth Amendment and classical sharia cannot share jurisdiction.

A FINAL WORD

There is something especially urgent about the topic of this chapter for American readers. The United States are a country that affirms freedom of conscience with respect to religion and other matters. There are more than 300,000 churches, tens of thousands of synagogues, thousands of mosques, Hindu temples, Buddhist centers, and houses of worship representing every faith tradition on earth. Americans of every religious background—and of no religious background—go to work together, live in the same neighborhoods, send their children to the same schools, and stand equal before the law.

That equality was built, deliberately and at great cost, into the architecture of the Constitution. It was reinforced, at the cost of many precious lives in the bloodiest war in American history, by the Fourteenth Amendment. It is protected daily by courts that take equal protection seriously as a constitutional constraint rather than mere abstract aspiration.

Classical sharia would undo and reverse the 14th Amendment. Not by accident, but as a deliberate expression of its foundational principle: Allah has assigned different legal values to different categories of human being,

Islam is supreme, Muslims are superior in legal standing to non-Muslims, and this hierarchy is not subject to human revision because it comes from Allah himself.

The Fourteenth Amendment was written to say: not here. Not in this country. Not under this Constitution. That is a principle worth understanding clearly—and defending without apology.

5

STONES, WHIPS, AND SEVERED HANDS—HOW SHARIA'S PRESCRIBED PUNISHMENTS VIOLATE THE EIGHTH AMENDMENT

There is a short sentence in the Eighth Amendment to the United States Constitution that has done more to define the boundaries of civilized governance than almost any other clause in the Bill of Rights: Excessive bail shall not be required, nor excessive fines imposed, nor cruel and unusual punishments inflicted. The last five words are the ones that matter most for this chapter. What are cruel and unusual punishments? The Founders did not define the phrase precisely—they did not need to. They were drawing on a long Anglo-American legal tradition that understood, intuitively and from experience, that there are forms of punishment so brutal, so degrading, so disproportionate to any legitimate penological purpose, that no human government may justly impose them on human beings.

The Supreme Court has developed that intuition into a substantial body of constitutional law. In *Trop v. Dulles* (1958), Chief Justice Earl Warren wrote that the Eighth Amendment "must draw its meaning from the evolving standards of decency that mark the progress of a maturing society." In case after case, the Court has asked whether a given punishment shocks the conscience of a civilized society—whether it degrades human dignity in ways that no legitimate governmental purpose can justify. Torture, barbaric mutilation, punishments grossly disproportionate to the offense—these are what the Eighth Amendment prohibits, and American courts have consistently enforced its prohibition.

Classical sharia has a different answer to the question of what punishments are appropriate. It has an entire category of punishments—called *hudud*, meaning "limits" or "boundaries"—that are prescribed directly by the Quran and the hadith, with fixed penalties that no human judge, no legislature, and no popular vote can reduce or set aside, because they come from Allah himself. These include amputation of the hand for theft, public flogging for drinking alcohol and for certain sexual offenses, stoning to death for adultery, and death—by various means, in various schools—for homosexuality.

Every one of these punishments would be struck down in American courts as an obvious, categorical violation of the Eighth Amendment—not a close question, not a matter requiring elaborate analysis of the prohibition on cruel and unusual punishment—a prohibition that exists precisely because free societies have decided that the power of the state over the human body has limits that governing authorities should not exceed

This chapter examines where the hudud punishments come from, what they look like when applied, and why they represent one of the most direct and irreconcilable conflicts between classical sharia and the United States Constitution.

WHAT HUDUD MEANS—AND WHY IT CANNOT BE REFORMED

The word hudud is the plural of *hadd*, meaning limit or boundary. In classical Islamic jurisprudence, the hudud are the punishments that Allah himself has prescribed for specific offenses—punishments that are, by definition, not subject to human modification. The finality and supremacy of Allah's rulings is the crucial distinction between Islamic criminal law and every other legal system in the modern world.

In American law, criminal penalties are set by legislatures, reviewed by courts, and subject to constitutional limits. They can be increased or decreased as society's understanding evolves. They can be challenged as disproportionate or inhumane. The democratic process and judicial review provide constant mechanisms for reform. No punishment is beyond challenge.

In classical sharia, the hudud are beyond challenge. They are not human legal choices. They are divine commands. The Quran prescribed them directly. Muhammad confirmed and applied them. The classical jurists systematized them. And because they derive from divine authority rather than human legislation, no caliph, no parliament, no constitutional court, and no popular vote can legitimately alter them. To reduce or abolish a hadd punishment is, in classical Islamic legal theory, to substitute human judgment for that of Allah—doing so is a form of *kufr* (infidelity) or *shirk* (polytheism) that Islam regards as the gravest of sins.

This reality is why debates about "reforming" Islamic criminal law are so theologically fraught within the Muslim world. A Muslim scholar who argues that stoning for adultery should be abolished is not merely proposing a legal reform. He is, from the perspective of classical sharia, claiming that his judgment about what is humane supersedes Allah's explicit command. That claim carries its own severe religious consequences.

For the purposes of the Eighth Amendment, such theological rigidity matters enormously. The constitutional prohibition on cruel and unusual punishment applies regardless of the source of the punishment—whether it comes from a secular legislature, a religious authority, or a claim of divine command. The source of the punishment does not change what it does to a human body. And what the hudud punishments do to human bodies is, by any standard that American constitutional law recognizes, cruel and unusual.

THE AMPUTATED HAND: THEFT'S PRESCRIBED PRICE

In Surah 5:38 the Quran prescribes, with brutal directness, amputation as the penalty for theft: "As for the thief, the male and the female, cut off their hands as punishment for what they committed as a deterrent from Allah."

Classical Islamic jurisprudence developed detailed conditions for when amputation applies—the stolen goods must reach a minimum value, the items stolen must have been taken from a secured location, and so forth. These conditions mean that not every petty theft triggers the hadd penalty. But once the conditions are met, the prescribed punishment becomes mandatory. No judge has discretion. No mitigating circumstances reduce it.

The hand is amputated—specifically the right hand, at the wrist—as Allah has commanded.

In Saudi Arabia, this punishment is applied to this day. Amputations for theft have been carried out in the Kingdom in the twenty-first century—documented, court-ordered, and religiously sanctioned. In Iran, the Islamic Republic has similarly carried out judicial amputations. In Sudan under Omar al-Bashir's Islamist government, amputations were performed. Under ISIS, which applied classical hudud punishments with systematic thoroughness in the territories it controlled in Iraq and Syria between 2014 and 2019, amputations were filmed and posted online as evidence of proper Islamic governance. Graphic videos of such penalties applied can be viewed online, and they are not medieval illustrations. They are twenty-first century documentation of a Quranic punishment being applied by people who believe, with complete sincerity and substantial jurisprudential support, that they are doing exactly what Allah commanded.

Imagine an American court being asked to uphold such a sentence. Picture a judge ordering the surgical removal of a convicted shoplifter's hand as a criminal penalty. The Eighth Amendment analysis would likely take less than thirty seconds: the punishment is mutilation, it is irreversible, it permanently marks the body of the convicted person in a way that cannot be undone by a subsequent finding of innocence, and it serves no penal purpose—rehabilitation, deterrence, incapacitation—that could not be served by imprisonment without the permanent physical destruction. American courts have struck down far less severe sentences as violations of the Eighth Amendment. Judicial amputation would not survive constitutional scrutiny.

THE LASH: PUBLIC FLOGGING FOR ALCOHOL AND SEX

In Surah 24:2, the Quran prescribes one hundred lashes for fornication—sexual intercourse outside of marriage: "The adulterer and the adulteress, flog each of them a hundred lashes, and let not compassion keep you from carrying out Allah's sentence, if you believe in Allah and the Last Day, and let a party of the faithful witness their punishment."

Note the embedded instruction: do not be taken by pity. The punishment is to be administered *without mercy*—and it is to be *witnessed publicly.*

Degradation is part of the sentence. Suffering before an audience is not incidental to the penalty. It is a core feature of the penalty.

The hadith adds the punishment of lashing for drinking alcohol—eighty lashes in the majority opinion of the classical schools, based on the practice of the early caliphs who derived the number from various prophetic traditions. Muhammad ordered floggings for alcohol consumption. The companions carried them out. And the jurists codified them into systems of law.

In Saudi Arabia, public flogging has long been a standard judicial punishment, applied for offenses ranging from alcohol consumption to sexual misconduct to—as in the case of Raif Badawi, discussed in Chapter Three—blogging. Badawi's sentence of one thousand lashes, to be administered fifty at a time every Friday, became internationally known precisely because its methodical, calculated brutality was impossible to mistake for anything other than torture, delivered in installments, and designed to maximize suffering over time while keeping the victim alive for the next session.

In Iran under the Islamic Republic, flogging is a routine judicial punishment for alcohol consumption, sexual offenses, and a range of other violations of Islamic moral law. In Afghanistan under the Taliban, public floggings have been carried out in sport stadiums before crowds of spectators—precisely as the Quran's instruction that there be witness to the punishment requires. These are not aberrations of the Taliban's unique brutality. They are the classical sharia punishment applied as its source prescribes.

The government of Pakistan also applies elements of classical sharia through its Hudood Ordinances—enacted in 1979 under General Zia ul-Haq's Islamization program. These ordinances prescribe flogging for alcohol and sexual offenses. Women have been flogged under these laws. The Hudood Ordinances became infamous internationally for the often impossible evidentiary standards they created for rape cases: a woman who alleged rape and cannot produce four male Muslim witnesses to the act may herself be charged with adultery or fornication—and flogged for it. The law effectively turns many or most rape victims who do not stay silent into potential criminals. Should a raped woman in a sharia court have to beg *four* Muslim men to come forward and testify that they witnessed her being raped to prove her innocence? Should she be forced to relive her trauma by desperately searching for male eyewitnesses who may not even exist?

Should her failure to produce these four witnesses result in her own punishment for "illicit sex" while her rapist walks free? This stipulation is not a misapplication of sharia. It is sharia's classical evidentiary requirements—four male Muslim witnesses for the hadd punishment of illicit sex (*zina*)—applied directly to rape cases. The result is that rape in most cases becomes impossible to prosecute, while the victim herself becomes legally vulnerable to false accusation and flogging. These rules flow straight from the Quran and hadith, and they reveal the profound injustice embedded in classical sharia when it comes to protecting women.

The Eighth Amendment's prohibition of cruel and unusual punishment has been applied by American courts to punishments far less severe than public flogging. The Supreme Court has held that prison conditions constituting "wanton and unnecessary infliction of pain" violate the Eighth Amendment. It has held that the use of excessive force by guards against prisoners is unconstitutional. It has held that sentences grossly disproportionate to the offense violate the cruel and unusual punishment clause. Judicial flogging—the deliberate, court-ordered infliction of physical pain on a human body as a criminal penalty—would not survive Eighth Amendment scrutiny in an American court.

DEATH BY STONING: THE PUNISHMENT THAT HAS NO DEFENSE

Of all the hudud punishments, stoning—*rajm* in Arabic—is the one that most brazenly defies constitutional standards. It is the most brutal, the most prolonged, and the most purposely agonizing form of execution in the classical sharia repertoire. It is prescribed for adultery, and it is applied—in the twenty-first century, in multiple countries—as an expression of divine will.

Stoning is not prescribed explicitly in the Quran for adultery (the Quranic penalty for fornication is flogging, as we have seen). Islam's prescription for stoning comes from the hadith, where it is documented with extensive detail in the most authoritative collections—here the hadith contradicts the Quran. In *Sahih al-Bukhari* and *Sahih Muslim*, there are multiple records of Muhammad personally ordering and supervising stoning as punishment for adultery. In one account, a woman from the tribe of Ghamid came to Muhammad confessing adultery and asking to be purified through punishment. Muhammad initially tried to send her away. She returned repeatedly, insisting on her confession. After she gave birth to the child of the adulterous relationship and weaned it, Muhammad had her stoned. The narration records that one of Muhammad's companions spat in her face during the stoning, and that Muhammad rebuked him—not for participating in her killing, but for presuming to judge her soul.

Islam's classical jurisprudence on stoning is extensively developed. The condemned person is to be partially buried—a woman to her waist, a man to his chest in some accounts—so as to be incapable of fleeing. Stones of a specific size range are prescribed—large enough to cause serious injury and eventual death, but small enough that death does not come too quickly. The execution is communal: members of the public are to participate in the killing. If a confession was used as—i.e., if there were no witnesses—then the first stone must be thrown by the judge. In contrast, if witnesses provided the evidence, they must throw the first stones.

These details are not figurative. They are a prescribed protocol for execution, derived from hadith, codified in *fiqh*, and applied in multiple countries across the centuries until today. Iran has carried out stonings in the twenty-first century. Saudi Arabia has sentenced individuals to stoning. Afghanistan under the Taliban has stoned people in public executions. Sudan has issued stoning sentences. In northern Nigeria, where twelve states adopted sharia criminal law in 1999 and 2000, stoning sentences have been issued, though international pressure has prevented some from being carried out.

The Supreme Court of the United States has held that execution by electrocution, if it causes unnecessary pain, may violate the Eighth Amendment. It has held that execution of juveniles and intellectually disabled individuals violates the Eighth Amendment categorically. It has engaged in extensive deliberation over whether specific lethal injection protocols cause sufficient pain to constitute cruel and unusual punishment. Against this backdrop, stoning—a method of execution that is expressly designed to be prolonged, communal, and agonizing, that buries its victim in the ground before killing him or her with thrown rocks, that involves the participation of crowds as an expression of collective moral judgment—does not present a close Eighth Amendment question. It is cruel. It is unusual. It would be unconstitutional in the United States in any court.

THE DEATH PENALTY FOR HOMOSEXUAL ACTS

Few aspects of classical sharia's criminal jurisprudence represent a more direct collision with American constitutional principles than its treatment of homosexuality. Americans themselves continue to debate, vigorously and in good faith, the proper scope of legal protections for same-sex relationships, the nature of marriage, and the appropriate boundaries of state recognition of private conduct. This book does not enter those debates and takes no position in them. What is not debated—and what the Constitution does not permit—is the execution of American citizens by the state for their private consensual conduct. Whatever one believes about the morality of homosexual practice or the wisdom of any particular Supreme Court decision, the American constitutional framework categorically prohibits the kind of lethal state violence that classical sharia prescribes for homosexual conduct. That prohibition represents an absolute and irreconcilable incompatibility between the two legal systems.

Under classical sharia, same-sex relations are not merely disapproved. They are a capital offense.

The Quranic basis for the condemnation of homosexuality draws on the story of Lot and the destruction of Sodom—a narrative that appears also in the Hebrew Bible—which Islamic tradition interprets as divine punishment of a people who practiced *liwat*, the Arabic term for male homosexual intercourse derived from Lot's name. Surah 7:80–81 records: "And Lot, when he said to his people, 'Do you commit such immorality as no one has preceded you with from among the worlds? Indeed, you come with lust upon men instead of women. Indeed, you are a transgressing people.'" The Quran does not explicitly prescribe a specific legal penalty for homosexuality, but its condemnation is unambiguous.

The hadith supplies the penalty. Muhammad is recorded in multiple hadith collections—including those of Abu Dawud, al-Tirmidhi, and Ibn Majah—as saying: "If you find anyone doing as Lot's people did, kill the one who does it and the one to whom it is done." Both parties to a homosexual act are to be killed.

The classical jurists elaborated this ruling with characteristic thoroughness. The Hanbali, Maliki, and Shafi'i schools prescribe death for the active partner in male homosexual intercourse, with debate about whether the passive partner receives the same penalty or a lesser one. The Hanafi school prescribes death in some circumstances and severe corporal punishment in others. There is variation in the prescribed method—some schools say stoning, others say throwing from a height, others say the sword—but there is no major classical school of Sunni jurisprudence that does not prescribe a severe physical penalty, and the dominant opinion in most schools is death. Contemporary courts and governments confirm it.

In Iran, the Islamic Republic has executed men for homosexuality since its founding in 1979. Human rights organizations have documented hundreds of cases. Homosexual men have been hanged from cranes in public squares. In 2005, two Iranian teenagers—Mahmoud Asgari, aged sixteen, and Ayaz Marhoni, aged eighteen—were publicly hanged in the city of Mashhad. Iranian authorities initially claimed they were executed for rape, but the case attracted international attention and human rights investigators concluded that the charges were related to consensual homosexual conduct.

In Saudi Arabia, homosexuality is punishable by flogging, imprisonment, and in some cases death. In Afghanistan under the Taliban, homosexual men have been executed. In the parts of Iraq and Syria controlled by ISIS, homosexual men were thrown from the rooftops of buildings—a method of execution derived from a minority jurisprudential opinion about the appropriate penalty for homosexuality—and then stoned if they survived the fall. These executions were filmed and disseminated as religious instruction.

In every country that applies classical sharia as its criminal law, the state itself becomes the instrument of lethal violence against people for their private conduct. This is not the product of individual prejudice or cultural tradition operating outside the law. It is the law.

The American constitutional framework operates from a categorically different premise. Whatever the ongoing debates about the proper scope of legal recognition for same-sex relationships—and those debates are genuine, significant, and unresolved among thoughtful Americans—the Constitution does not permit the state to execute, imprison, or inflict physical punishment on citizens for their private consensual conduct. That principle is not a recent invention. It reflects a foundational commitment to the limits of state power over individual persons that runs through the constitutional order from its origins. When the American people or their courts have fallen short of that commitment—as they have at various points in the nation's history—the constitutional framework has provided mechanisms for correction and reform. That capacity for self-correction, grounded in popular sovereignty and constitutional principle, is itself something that sharia's claim to eternal divine command cannot accommodate.

Classical sharia does not merely occupy a different position on the spectrum of legal approaches to homosexuality. It occupies a different universe—one in which the state is commanded by divine law to kill. There is no reading of the relevant hadith that removes the death penalty. There is no interpretation of classical fiqh that transforms the execution of homosexual men into a metaphor. The text says what it says. The jurists ruled as they ruled. The countries applying these laws are doing what the tradition requires. That requirement is incompatible with the American constitutional order—not because every American agrees about the nature of marriage or the morality of homosexual practice, but because no version of the American constitutional framework permits the state to prescribe death for private consensual conduct between adults.

THE EIGHTH AMENDMENT'S VISION

The Eighth Amendment is, at its deepest level, a statement about human dignity. It says that no matter what a person has done, no matter how serious the offense, the state may not treat the human body as an object to be mutilated, tortured, or destroyed in any way the government chooses. The person convicted of the worst crimes retains a fundamental human dignity that the state must respect—not because the criminal deserves compassion, but because a society that tortures and mutilates its criminals has degraded itself, not just its prisoners. This understanding of human dignity flows directly from the biblical teaching that every human being is created in the *imago Dei*—the image of God (Genesis 1:26–27). In the Judeo-Christian worldview that shaped America's founding, even the worst offender still bears the imprint of God's likeness, which no government has the right to deface through cruel or degrading punishments.

That vision of human dignity is completely absent from classical sharia's hudud jurisprudence. The hudud punishments are not designed with the dignity of the offender in mind. They are designed with the superiority of Allah's command in mind—and in that framework, the suffering of the human body is not a cost to be minimized but a feature of the punishment's divine legitimacy. The more clearly the punishment demonstrates God's absolute authority over human conduct, the more perfectly it fulfills its purpose.

Amputation leaves a permanent, visible mark on the body—a constant reminder to the amputee and to everyone who sees him that he was found guilty before God's law. Public flogging degrades the offender before the community—stripping him of privacy and dignity as part of the sentence. Stoning kills communally—making the entire community complicit in the enforcement of God's law. Death for homosexuality eliminates from the community those whose existence Allah has declared an abomination.

The Eighth Amendment declares: not in this country. It says that whatever theological framework a religion may employ, the state may not use it as a basis for mutilating, torturing, or killing human beings. It says that human dignity places limits on state power that no claimed divine mandate can override.

That principle is not negotiable. It is not subject to religious exception. It applies equally to Christian, Jewish, and Islamic claims of divine authority over criminal punishment. And it places the hudud fixed penalties of classical sharia—amputation, flogging, stoning, death for homosexuality—permanently and irreconcilably outside the bounds of what the United States Constitution permits.

WHAT YOU WILL HEAR—AND WHY IT DOES NOT HOLD UP

Defenders of sharia in Western contexts typically respond to the hudud punishments with one of two arguments.

The first is that the evidentiary requirements for hudud punishments are so strict—four male Muslim witnesses to the act of adultery, for example—that they are practically never applied, and therefore the punishments are more symbolic than real. This argument requires ignoring the documented record of hudud punishments being applied in Saudi Arabia, Iran, Afghanistan, Nigeria, and elsewhere in the twenty-first century. It requires ignoring that the evidentiary standards, while strict for adultery, are far less stringent for other offenses, and that confession—which Islamic courts have historically obtained through coercion—can substitute for witness testimony. Most fundamentally, it requires accepting that the appropriate constitutional response to a prescribed punishment is "it's rarely applied"—a standard that no American court has ever accepted as a substitute for constitutional compliance. A law that prescribes amputation for theft does not become constitutionally acceptable because its prosecutors rarely prove their cases.

The second argument is that these punishments should be understood as cultural expressions of a different civilization's values, and that Western criticism of them is a form of cultural imperialism or 'Islamophobia.' This argument, however, collapses under its own weight. The Eighth Amendment does not prohibit cruel and unusual punishment only in Western cultures. It prohibits the infliction of such punishments by the government of the United States—and by extension, it prohibits any parallel legal system operating within the United States from applying them. Cultural relativism is not a constitutional defense. The human body does not hurt differently depending on the civilization doing the cutting.

CONCLUSION

The Eighth Amendment and classical sharia represent two completely different answers to the question of what the state may do to the human body in the name of justice. The Eighth Amendment says the state's power over the body is limited by human dignity—a dignity that belongs to every person regardless of their offense. Classical sharia says Allah's power over the body is unlimited—that the prescribed penalties express divine will and that human dignity is not a constraint on their application.

Amputated hands. Flogged backs. Bodies buried to the waist and stoned to death. Homosexual men thrown from rooftops. These are not hypothetical horrors. They are the twenty-first century application of a legal system that has remained structurally unchanged since the seventh century—because its adherents believe, with genuine theological sincerity, that changing it would be to set human judgment above Allah's.

America has decided otherwise. The Eighth Amendment is its answer—clear, categorical, and non-negotiable.

6

WE THE PEOPLE VS. WE THE BELIEVERS—WHY SHARIA'S DIVINE SOVEREIGNTY CANNOT COEXIST WITH AMERICAN DEMOCRACY

On the very first line of the United States Constitution, you will find three words that changed the history of human governance forever: We the People. Not We the Monarchy. Not We the Church. Not We the Generals, the Aristocrats, the Priests, or the Prophets. We the People—a plain, unprecedented declaration that the authority of this government derives from the consent of ordinary human beings, and from nothing else.

Those three words were revolutionary when they were penned in 1787 and they remain revolutionary today—because most of human history has been governed by a different principle. For most of recorded civilization, political authority claimed not merely divine sanction but exclusive divine mandate — a claim that placed the ruler beyond human accountability. Kings ruled not merely by God's providence but by God's specific appointment, answerable to no earthly assembly. Priests legislated not merely in keeping with divine teaching but as its exclusive interpreters, beyond challenge. Conquerors governed not merely under divine permission but as instruments of divine will that no human verdict could reverse. The pattern was consistent: whoever claimed to speak for the deity above claimed a power that no human vote, no popular assembly, and no constitutional amendment could legitimately override—because the people's judgment was irrelevant before God's.

The American Founders looked at that history and made a different choice. They located political sovereignty in the people—fallible, diverse, disagreeing, arguing people—and they built a system of government designed to translate that popular sovereignty into law through elections, legislation, and a Constitution that the people themselves could amend. No divine mandate. No sacred text with the force of law. No prophet whose commands supersede the vote of the legislature. The people govern themselves, and the law belongs to them.

Classical sharia arrives at a different conclusion because it begins from a different premise. It locates ultimate political sovereignty not in the people but in Allah (or, more proximally, Muhammad's revelation)—and it means this not as a spiritual sentiment but as a constitutional principle with concrete legal consequences. In classical Islamic political theory, the people do not govern themselves. Allah governs. His law—revealed in the Quran, demonstrated in the life of Muhammad, elaborated by the jurists—is the only legitimate source of political authority. Democracy, in this framework, is not a *different* form of government. It is a form of idolatry.

This chapter is about that conflict—why it is the deepest and most fundamental incompatibility between sharia and the American constitutional order, and why it cannot be resolved by compromise, reinterpretation, or goodwill.

HAKIMIYYA: ALLAH'S SOVEREIGNTY AS CONSTITUTIONAL PRINCIPLE

The Arabic word that encapsulates classical Islam's political theology is *hakimiyya*—divine sovereignty. The word comes from the Arabic root *h-k-m*, meaning to govern, to judge, to rule. In classical Islamic thought, *hakimiyya* belongs exclusively and completely to Allah. He alone governs. He alone judges. He alone has the absolute and legitimate authority to make law.

This idea is not peripheral in Islamic political thought. It is its foundation. The Quran states it directly in multiple verses. Surah 12:40 declares: "Judgment [or Legislation, Arabic, *al-ḥukm*] belongs only to Allah. He has commanded that you worship none but him." Surah 6:57 states: "The decision is only for Allah." Surah 5:44 warns: "Whoever does not judge by what Allah has revealed—those are the infidels." Surah 5:45 continues: "Whoever does not judge by what Allah has revealed—those are the wrongdoers." Surah 5:47 adds: "Whoever does not judge by what Allah has revealed—those are the rebelliously disobedient."

Three essentially consecutive verses designate three categories of condemnation—disbeliever, wrongdoer, defiantly disobedient—for the act of governing by something other than Allah's revealed law. The message is not subtle. Any system of governance that derives its authority from human rather than divine sources is, in this Quranic framework, an act of rebellion against God.

The twentieth-century Islamist thinker Sayyid Qutb (1906–1966)—an Egyptian member of the Muslim Brotherhood who was executed by Gamal Abdel Nasser's government in 1966 and whose writings remain among the most widely read in Islamist circles worldwide—built his entire political theology on these verses. In his landmark work *Milestones*, which has been described as the manifesto of modern Islamist radicalism, Qutb argued that most of the world—including Muslim-majority societies that had adopted secular constitutions—was living in a state of *jahiliyya*: the pre-Islamic barbarism and ignorance that Islam came to replace. Democracy, in Qutb's analysis, is *jahiliyya* institutionalized. It is the formal, systematic substitution of human sovereignty for divine sovereignty—the collective act of placing human beings in the position that belongs only to Allah.

Qutb did not invent this argument. He derived it from the works of jurist Abu al-Ala Mawdudi (1903–1979), the Pakistani Islamic scholar who coined the modern use of the term *hakimiyya* in its political sense and who argued, with meticulous theological reasoning, that Islam is inherently incompatible with democracy because democracy places legislative authority in human hands while Islam places it exclusively in Allah's hands. Mawdudi's works are taught in Islamic universities. His arguments are cited in the founding documents of Islamist organizations worldwide. His influence on contemporary Islamist political thought cannot be overstated.

This worldview is not fringe theology. It is the logical development of Quranic verses that have been part of Islamic orthodoxy for fourteen centuries, applied to the specific question of modern democratic governance. And neither is *Milestones* a text confined to the extremist fringe. It has been translated into virtually every language Muslims read. Its influence crosses the Sunni-Shiʿi divide—the Farsi translation was made by none other than Ayatollah Khamenei, who served as Supreme Leader of Iran from 1989 until his death in 2026. To understand political Islam in the twenty-first century is, in large part, to understand this book.

DEMOCRACY IS *SHIRK*: THE THEOLOGICAL ARGUMENT

To fully grasp how deep the conflict between classical Islam and self-governance goes, an American reader needs to understand one more Arabic term: *shirk*. In Islamic theology, *shirk* is the gravest possible sin—the association of partners with Allah, the attribution of divine qualities or divine authority to anything other than Allah. In fact, it is the one sin, according to mainstream Islamic theology, that Allah will not forgive. Surah 4:48 states: "Indeed, Allah does not forgive association with him, but he forgives what is less than that for whom he wills."

Now consider what happens when classical Islamic political theology is applied to democracy. In a democracy, human beings make laws through representatives they have elected. They assemble in legislatures and decide what is permitted and what is prohibited. They make collective decisions about morality, social organization, criminal punishment, and public life. In doing so, they are—from the perspective of classical *hakimiyya* doctrine—claiming for themselves the legislative authority that belongs, in Muhammad's vision, exclusively to Allah. They are, in this framework, committing *shirk*—not in the personal, private sense of worshipping an idol, but in the political and legal sense of attributing divine sovereignty to human institutions.

That conclusion is the explicit argument of serious Islamic scholars. When Islamist preachers tell their congregants that voting in a democratic election is *haram*—religiously forbidden—or that participating in a secular legislative process is a form of *shirk*, they are not speaking without a foundation. They are making a precise theological argument that has deep roots in the Islamic legal tradition. When online Islamist forums describe democracy as "the rule of man over man" and contrast it with the "rule of Allah over man" that sharia represents, they are applying a framework that Mawdudi and Qutb systematized but that the Quran itself provided.

Browse any social media platform where Islamist content circulates and you will find this argument made constantly, in dozens of languages, to audiences of millions. "Democracy is *shirk*." "Voting is *haram*." "The Constitution is man-made; the Quran is from Allah." "We don't need elections; we need the sharia." These are not the ravings of isolated extremists. They are the popular expression of a theological position that has respectable scholarly pedigree and that represents, for a significant portion of the world's Islamist population, the obvious and necessary conclusion of Islamic political theology.

MUHAMMAD'S POLITICAL MODEL: THE ANTI-DEMOCRATIC TEMPLATE

The Islamist argument against democracy is not merely theological. It is also historical—grounded in the political model that Muhammad himself established and that classical sharia requires Muslims to imitate.

Muhammad did not govern Medina through popular consent. He governed it through divine command. His authority derived not from the *islam* (submission) of his followers and from his status as Allah's messenger—the channel through which divine will be revealed to humanity. When Muhammad decided—about law, about war, about punishment, about governance—that decision was binding not because the community had voted on it but because Allah had spoken through his prophet. The Quran makes this doctrine explicit in Surah 33:36: "It is not for a believing man or a believing woman, when Allah and his Messenger have decided a matter, that they should have any choice in their matter." No choice. When Allah and his Messenger have decided, the matter is settled. The community does not vote. The community does not deliberate and reach a different conclusion. It obeys.

After Muhammad's death, the early Islamic community was governed by the caliphs—his successors as political and religious leaders of the Muslim community. The caliph's authority was not democratic. It was not derived from popular election in any modern sense. It was derived from his role as guardian of the sharia and leader of the umma—the community of Muslims. His obligation was not to represent the preferences of the people but to implement the law of Allah. This claim is why, after Muhammad's death, when many Arab tribes abandoned Islam or refused to submit to the new authority, his successor Abu Bakr launched the *Ridda* (i.e., "Apostasy") Wars. He fought to forcibly restore the tribes to Islam or, when they resisted, to subdue or massacre them without mercy, thereby reasserting the supremacy of divine law over any individual or tribal consent.

The classical Islamic political tradition never developed a concept of popular sovereignty because it never needed one. Sovereignty belonged to Allah. The caliph's legitimacy came not not from the consent of the governed, but from his fidelity to divine law. Consultation (*shura*) was valued in Islamic political theory, but it was advisory, not legislative—the community could offer counsel, but it could not change what Allah had revealed or dictated.

Islamist movements seek to restore this political model—not a theocracy in the loose sense of a government influenced by religious values, but a theocracy in the precise sense of a government that derives its authority from divine law, enforces that law through religious institutions, and regards any deviation from it as not merely politically wrong but cosmically sinful.

"WE THE PEOPLE" VS. "WE THE BELIEVERS"

The Preamble to the United States Constitution opens with seven words that are among the most consequential in the history of political thought: We the People of the United States. The Constitution then proceeds to establish a government whose every power derives from that source—the people. The legislature is elected by the people. The President is chosen through a process accountable to the people. The courts interpret laws made by the people's representatives. And the Constitution itself can be amended by the people—through a demanding process designed to ensure broad consensus, but a human process, not a divine one.

This phrase means something profound and specific: no provision of the United States Constitution is beyond human revision. The First Amendment can theoretically be amended. The Eighth Amendment can theoretically be amended. The Fourteenth Amendment—which was itself an amendment—can theoretically be amended again. The process is deliberately difficult. But it is possible, because the Constitution rests on the authority of the people, and the people retain the ultimate power to change their own governing framework.

Classical sharia offers no such possibility. The Quran cannot be amended. The hadith cannot be revised. The rulings of the classical jurists, insofar as they derive from these divine sources, cannot be democratically overturned. A Muslim legislature that voted to abolish the hudud punishments, or to grant equal legal standing to non-Muslims, or to permit Muslims to leave Islam without penalty, would not be exercising popular sovereignty. It would be—in the framework of classical sharia—committing infidelity and apostasy at a national scale, substituting human judgment for divine command.

Herein lies the deepest incompatibility between sharia and the American constitutional order. It is not merely that specific sharia rules conflict with specific constitutional provisions—though they do, as every previous chapter has shown. It is that the two systems rest on completely different and mutually exclusive theories of where legitimate authority comes from.

The Constitution says: legitimate authority comes from the people, who may govern themselves as they choose within the limits they themselves establish.

Classical sharia says: legitimate authority comes from Allah, who has already established the limits, and the people have no authority to change them. These are diametrically opposed answers to the most fundamental question in political philosophy: who governs?

HEGEMONY, NOT PLURALISM

There is another dimension of the incompatibility that deserves direct attention. The American constitutional system is built on the principle of pluralism—the idea that a free society contains many different communities, beliefs, and ways of life, and that, so long as they do not infringe anyone else's God-given rights, the law's role is to protect each of them equally rather than to favor any one of them.

Classical sharia does not operate on the principle of pluralism. It operates on the principle of Islamic hegemony—the supremacy of Islamic governance over all other systems.

The classical Islamic division of the world into *dar al-Islam* (the house of Islam, governed by sharia) and *dar al-harb* (the house of war, not yet governed by sharia) is not merely a descriptive geographical classification. It is a statement about the ultimate goal of Islamic political order: the entire world should eventually be governed by sharia. The *dar al-harb* is not a permanent condition to be accepted and respected. It is a temporary condition to be transformed. The obligation of the Muslim community—the umma—is to expand the *dar al-Islam* until it encompasses the world.

This goal is not fringe Islamism. It is classical Islamic theology, derived from Muhammad's own commands and from the Quranic obligation of dawah—calling people to convert to Islam—and jihad—the struggle to make Allah's word and rule supreme on earth. Muhammad himself sent letters to the rulers of neighboring empires—Persia, Byzantium, Egypt—calling them to accept Islam or face war, stating, "Accept Islam and you will be spared." He was not inviting them to a pluralist dialogue. He was presenting them with a demand: submit to Allah's sovereignty, which means submitting to Islamic dominance and governance.

The modern Islamist expression of this principle is more sophisticated but structurally identical. What differs is that, rather than military conquest—impractical in the current geopolitical environment—Islamist movements in the West pursue what they describe as a long-term project of dawah and political engagement: expanding the influence of Islamic values in law, policy, education, and culture, incrementally, until the society has been sufficiently transformed to accept sharia-compatible governance. The Muslim Brotherhood's 1991 internal document describing its mission as "eliminating and destroying Western civilization from within" is the explicit statement of a strategy that its authors regarded as the faithful application of classical Islamic political theology. Some describe this strategy as the modern jihad, as compared to the classical jihad of the early Muslim military expeditions and conquests.

This objective is not pluralism seeking a seat at the table. It is a competing sovereignty seeking to replace the table itself.

THE AMENDMENT PROCESS: DEMOCRACY'S SELF-CORRECTION MECHANISM

One of the most elegant features of the American constitutional system is its amendment process—the mechanism by which the people can correct their own mistakes, adapt their governing framework to changing circumstances, and expand the circle of constitutional protection over time. The abolition of slavery through the Thirteenth Amendment. The extension of equal protection through the Fourteenth. Women's suffrage through the Nineteenth. The direct election of senators through the Seventeenth. Each amendment represents the people using their sovereign power to adapt their own Constitution to more modern understandings.

This process assumes something that classical sharia categorically denies: that human beings have the authority and the wisdom to improve their own governing framework through collective deliberation and consent. The amendment process is an act of popular sovereignty—the people saying, in effect, "we made a mistake, or times have changed, or our understanding has shifted, and we are going to change our law accordingly."

Classical sharia regards this kind of human self-governance with theological suspicion at best and outright condemnation at worst. If Allah has already revealed the perfect law—and classical Islamic theology holds that he has—then the project of human beings deliberating about how to improve it is not democratic progress. It is presumption. It is the creature telling the Creator that his law needs revision. It is, in the framework of *hakimiyya*, a political form of *shirk*.

This stance is why Islamist movements in the West have a deeply ambivalent relationship with democratic participation. On one hand, they use democratic processes strategically—voting, running for office, lobbying, litigating—because these tools are available and effective for advancing their political goals in the current environment. On the other hand, they cannot, without theological contradiction, fully embrace democracy as a legitimate system of governance, because doing so would require accepting that human beings have the right to make and unmake law—including Islamic law—through popular consent. Some Islamist scholars have attempted to resolve this tension by arguing that Muslims may participate in democracy as a *temporary tactical* measure while working toward the long-term goal of establishing final Islamic governance. Others have argued that any participation in democratic institutions is *haram*. But both positions share the same underlying premise: democracy is not the legitimate permanent form of Islamic governance. It is at best a tool and at worst a sin.

THE CALIPHATE DREAM: WHAT ISLAMISTS ACTUALLY WANT

When Islamists speak openly about their political vision—as they do, frequently, in internal documents, theological writings, and online forums—they describe not a reformed democracy with Islamic values but a restored caliphate: a global Islamic state governed by sharia, led by a caliph who derives his authority from divine law rather than popular election, and encompassing eventually the entire umma—the global community of Muslims.

This dream is not the fantasy of a fringe. The restoration of the caliphate—abolished by Mustafa Kemal Atatürk when he dissolved the Ottoman caliphate in 1924—has been a central goal of the Muslim Brotherhood since its founding in 1928. It was the stated goal of al-Qaeda. It was the specific achievement that ISIS claimed when it declared its caliphate in 2014—a declaration that drew tens of thousands of recruits from dozens of countries, including the United States, precisely because it resonated with a deep aspiration in Islamist political theology.

The men and women who traveled from Western democracies to join ISIS were not, in most cases, people who had no understanding of what they were leaving behind. Many of them had grown up in democratic societies. They had attended democratic schools. They had benefited from democratic legal protections. And they chose to leave all of that for a seventh-century Arabian political model administered through public executions, slavery, and systematic terror—because that model claimed to represent the sovereignty of Allah rather than the sovereignty of fallible human beings.

That choice should tell us something important. The appeal of Islamic governance—of *hakimiyya* in its full, uncompromised form—is not merely the appeal of nostalgia or tribalism. It is the appeal of certainty: the conviction that there is a perfect law, that Allah has mandated and revealed it, that human imperfection and human disagreement can be replaced by divine clarity. Democracy, with its endless arguments and imperfect compromises and inevitable failures, looks shabby by comparison to people who believe that Allah has already provided the answer.

Although in a different context, the Constitution's framers understood the appeal of clerical rule, and deliberately built a system that resisted it. They were suspicious of unreflective certainty. They were suspicious of concentrated power—especially power that claimed divine sanction. They built a system of checks and balances, separation of powers, and guaranteed rights precisely to prevent any single authority—religious, political, or military—from claiming the kind of total governance that *hakimiyya* describes.

Their suspicion was well founded in human experience. Most societies in history that placed divine sovereignty above popular sovereignty have ended the same way: with a small group of self-appointed interpreters of divine will in possession of absolute, unaccountable power over everyone else.

WHAT AMERICANS MUST UNDERSTAND

The conflict between sharia's divine sovereignty and the Constitution's popular sovereignty is not merely a theoretical disagreement between political philosophers. It has practical, immediate implications for the American political project.

Islamist organizations operating in the United States understand the conflict well—and they have developed a sophisticated strategy for navigating it with a purpose or replacing rule by the people with rule by Allah. They participate in democratic politics while rejecting democracy's foundational premise. They invoke constitutional rights while working toward a goal that would eliminate those rights. They frame their project in the language of religious freedom, civil rights, and multicultural inclusion—and they rely upon the fact that most Americans do not understand Islamic political theology well enough to recognize the contradiction.

When a Muslim political candidate argues for sharia-compatible policies in a democratic legislature, he is using democratic tools to advance an anti-democratic theology. When an Islamist advocacy organization invokes the First Amendment to protect its activities, it is using a constitutional right to undermine the constitutional order in which that right is embedded. When Islamic studies programs at American universities—funded by Qatari and Saudi wealth—teach students that sharia and democracy are compatible, they are producing graduates who will carry that false comfort into institutions of influence across American society.

The compatibility argument is false. Not slightly overstated. Not true in some contexts and false in others. *False*—as a matter of political theology, as a matter of jurisprudential history, and as a matter of the explicit, documented goals of the Islamist movements that are advancing it. Classical sharia and American democracy rest on mutually exclusive premises about the source of legitimate authority. Sharia says Allah governs. The Constitution says the people govern. These premises cannot both be true at the same time, in the same society, under the same legal framework. One must yield to the other.

The answer is already written into the first three words of the Constitution—and it rests on a principle that *hakimiyya* directly and comprehensively denies: that no human being, no institution, and no self-appointed spokesman for divine will possesses the kind of absolute, unaccountable authority that only God could legitimately hold. The Founders built their entire system around that recognition. They were not hostile to the divine. They were suspicious of anyone who claimed to govern in its name—because they had seen, from bitter experience, where that claim always leads. That is not an insult to God. It is the wisdom of people who understood, from human experience, what happens when any institution—synagogue, church, mosque, caliphate, or crown—claims to govern in God's name.

CONCLUSION: THE SOVEREIGNTY THAT CANNOT BE SHARED

Sovereignty cannot be divided between Allah and the people. It cannot be shared between Quran and Constitution. It cannot be split between caliph and Congress. These are not different expressions of the same underlying political value. They are competing claims to ultimate authority—and ultimately, one must prevail.

The United States Constitution settled this question for the nation in 1787 and has defended the answer through every challenge since. The answer is popular sovereignty—government of the people, by the people, for the people, accountable to the people, and amendable by the people. No divine mandate overrides it. The Bible may inform it, but no sacred text supersedes it. No prophet's command replaces it.

Classical sharia's answer is the opposite: divine sovereignty—unquestionable, unappealable, unchangeable government of Allah, by Allah's law, for Allah's glory, through Allah's caliph, accountable to Allah's jurists, and not amendable by any human assembly regardless of how many people consent. The people's consent is irrelevant, as Allah has already spoken.

Between these two answers, there is no middle ground. There is no constitutional accommodation that can honor both simultaneously. There is no legal framework that can say both "We the People" and "Judgment belongs only to Allah" without lying to one of them.

America made her choice in 1776. She made it in Philadelphia in 1787, confirmed it in blood between 1861 and 1865, and has reaffirmed it in every generation since. The choice is popular sovereignty — imperfect, contentious, perpetually argued over, and messy. Sharia offers a different choice. Americans should understand exactly what that choice is — and why it leads somewhere that no free people should ever want to go. As America enters her two hundred and fifty-first year, that understanding has never mattered more.

7

ONE LAW FOR ALL—WHY AMERICA CANNOT ACCOMMODATE A PARALLEL LEGAL ORDER THAT SUBORDINATES ITS OWN CITIZENS

There is a principle so basic to the American legal tradition that, until recently, most citizens have never had to articulate it, because it has never seriously been challenged: in the United States, there is one legal system. One system of courts. One body of constitutional rights. One framework of law that applies equally to every person within its jurisdiction, regardless of their religion, their ethnicity, their community, or their private beliefs. You may belong to any faith you choose. You may organize your personal life according to any religious tradition you find meaningful. But when a legal dispute arises—when rights are claimed, when wrongs are remedied, when the coercive power of the state is invoked—there is only one law, and it applies to everyone.

This principle is not hostile to religion. It is, in fact, religion's greatest protection, because the one law that applies to everyone is a law that protects everyone equally—including religious minorities whose beliefs and practices the majority might find strange, offensive, or threatening. The Baptist who fears a Catholic court; the Jew who fears a Protestant legislature; the Muslim who fears a Christian magistrate—all of them are protected by a single constitutional framework that refuses to let any religious community's law become the law of the land without the people's blessing.

That protection works in every direction—or it works in no direction. A constitutional system that protects religious minorities from majority religious imposition must also protect everyone from minority religious imposition. The same principle that prevents a Christian theocracy prevents an Islamic one. The same clause that protects Muslims from a government-established Christianity protects Christians, Jews, atheists, and Muslims themselves from a government-enforced sharia.

This chapter is about the specific challenge that sharia poses to that one-law principle—how it is being advanced in the United States today, what happens when it is given legal recognition, and why the Constitution permits religious practice but cannot permit a competing political-legal order that subordinates some citizens to others on the basis of their faith.

WHAT THE CONSTITUTION DOES ALLOW

Let us begin with clarity about what the Constitution genuinely permits—because the argument for sharia accommodation in America almost always begins by misrepresenting this concept.

The Constitution fully protects private religious practice. A Muslim may pray five times a day, fast during Ramadan, give *zakat* (alms), perform the *hajj* (pilgrimage), attend a mosque's gatherings, read the Quran, raise children in the Islamic tradition, wear religiously mandated clothing, abstain from alcohol and pork, and organize every dimension of his personal life according to Islamic teaching. None of this religious expression requires any constitutional accommodation beyond the baseline protection that the Free Exercise Clause already provides. These are personal religious practices, and the government has no business interfering with them.

The Constitution also permits voluntary religious arbitration. Parties to a dispute—in commercial matters, in some family law contexts, in community disagreements—may agree to submit their dispute to a religious tribunal and be bound by its ruling. Jewish *beth din* courts have operated in the United States for generations, resolving commercial and civil disputes between parties who *voluntarily* choose rabbinical arbitration. Catholic canon law governs internal Church matters. Protestant denominations have their own disciplinary processes. These are legitimate exercises of private voluntary association—people choosing to resolve their disputes through religious frameworks they share.

The key word is *voluntary*. The key concept is *private*. And the critical condition is that the outcome must not violate the constitutional rights of either party. A Jewish couple may submit their divorce to a *beth din*, but neither party can be denied their constitutional rights as a result. A Christian employee may agree to resolve a workplace dispute through church arbitration, but the arbitration cannot strip her of her statutory employment rights. Religious arbitration operates as a supplement to the civil legal system, not as a replacement for it—and it operates only when both parties genuinely and freely consent.

This framework is where sharia arbitration, as it has been advanced in several Western countries, and as Islamist organizations are promoting it in the United States, crosses a constitutional line. Not because it is Islamic. The reason is not hostility to Islam or to Muslim dispute resolution. It is that classical sharia—in its treatment of women, non-Muslims, apostates, and anyone who invokes rights that sharia does not recognize—produces outcomes that violate constitutional rights. And because the pressure that Muslim communities sometimes apply to ensure that members submit to sharia arbitration rather than civil courts, their participation is not always, or even usually, genuinely voluntary.

THE BRITISH WARNING: WHAT PARALLEL LEGAL SYSTEMS PRODUCE

The United States does not need to speculate about what happens when sharia arbitration is given formal or semi-formal legal recognition. It can look at Britain, which has traveled further down that road and has begun to experience the results.

In 2008, the Archbishop of Canterbury, Rowan Williams, suggested in a widely reported lecture that the incorporation of some aspects of sharia into British law might be "unavoidable"—that recognizing a degree of legal pluralism for Muslim communities could promote social harmony. The public reaction to his remarks was swift and largely negative, but the sharia tribunal infrastructure that Williams was gesturing toward was already well established.

Already by the time Williams spoke, there were dozens of sharia councils operating across Britain—some of them registered as arbitration tribunals under the Arbitration Act of 1996, others operating informally but with significant authority in their communities. These councils handled family law matters—primarily divorces, custody disputes, and inheritance questions—applying classical sharia principles to cases brought before them.

The results had been extensively documented by researchers, journalists, and human rights organizations, and they were not positive. Women who appeared before sharia councils seeking Islamic divorces—which require the husband's consent under classical sharia in a way that civil divorces do not—frequently found themselves pressured to accept settlements that civil courts would never have approved. Custody arrangements giving fathers presumptive authority over children, consistent with classical sharia's male guardianship (*wilaya*) doctrine, were reached in settings where women did not fully understand that they had the right to pursue different outcomes in civil courts. Inheritance disputes were resolved according to the sharia formula that gives daughters half the share of sons—outcomes that British civil law, which makes no distinction between sons and daughters in inheritance, would never have sanctioned.

Perhaps most troublingly, the "voluntary" nature of sharia council proceedings was frequently more theoretical than actual. In tight-knit Muslim communities where the social pressure to resolve disputes through Islamic institutions was intense, where women were told by religious authorities that civil divorce was not a real divorce in Allah's eyes, and where the consequences of defying community norms were severe, the freedom to choose a civil court was practically absent. Women were effectively coerced into sharia proceedings and bound by their outcomes—not by law, but by social and cultural community pressure that the existence of formal sharia institutions made more powerful.

A 2016 review commissioned by the British government—the Casey Review—found that sharia councils were, in practice, discriminating against women and operating as a parallel legal system that undermined the very rights the civil legal system was designed to protect. The review's author, Dame Louise Casey, was unambiguous: "There is only one law in this land, and that is British law." The parallel sharia system was not supplementing British law. Rather, it was competing with it—and in that competition, those with the least power in Muslim communities were losing.

The British example is the documented, real-world result of giving sharia arbitration formal or semi-formal legal recognition. It is Britain's experience, and it is a warning that Americans should take seriously.

SHARIA ARBITRATION IN THE UNITED STATES: THE ADVANCE

The push for sharia arbitration recognition in the United States is real, organized, and ongoing. It today operates through several channels simultaneously.

The first channel is direct advocacy—Islamist organizations arguing that Muslim Americans should be able to resolve family law disputes through Islamic tribunals, and that civil courts should enforce their outcomes as a contractual matter. The Fiqh Council of North America, which functions as a kind of fatwa-issuing body for North American Muslims, has issued guidance on Islamic divorce, inheritance, and family law matters that is applied by some American Muslims as binding religious law. Imam-led dispute resolution panels today operate in mosques across the country, handling matters ranging from commercial disagreements to divorce settlements.

The second channel is litigation—cases in which parties who have agreed to sharia arbitration seek civil court enforcement of the resulting rulings, or in which sharia principles are invoked in defense of conduct that civil law would otherwise regulate. American courts have, in various jurisdictions, been asked to enforce sharia arbitration agreements, to apply Islamic law to inheritance disputes, and to recognize Islamic marriage and divorce contracts.

The third channel is perhaps the most dangerous to target societies: the gradual normalization of sharia-compatible outcomes through social pressure, institutional accommodation, and the progressive reframing of sharia recognition as a civil rights issue. When Muslim advocacy organizations argue that refusing to recognize sharia arbitration is discrimination against Muslims, they are attempting to recruit the constitutional protection for religious freedom as a tool for dismantling the constitutional protection for equal rights. The argument is sophisticated and designed to make Americans feel that opposing parallel sharia jurisdiction is bigotry—when in fact it is the defense of the equal protection principle that protects everyone, including Muslim women and non Muslims who would be subjected to sharia's legal hierarchies and dictates.

THE WOMAN IN THE SHARIA COURT

The human cost of parallel sharia jurisdiction is grave. It has a face—many faces—and they are almost always women's faces.

Consider a Muslim American woman—let's call her Fatima, though her real name could be anything—who was married in a ceremony that included both a civil marriage license and an Islamic *nikah* contract. The *nikah* designated a *mahr*—a bride gift—and included provisions consistent with classical sharia regarding the husband's rights over the wife's movement, social activities, and religious practice. When the marriage broke down, the husband refused to grant an Islamic divorce—a *talaq*—without Fatima's agreement to forfeit her mahr and to accept a custody arrangement giving him primary authority over their children.

Fatima had every right under American civil law to obtain a divorce without her husband's consent, to pursue equitable distribution of marital assets, and to seek a custody arrangement based upon the best interests of the children—the standard that American family courts apply without regard to the religious preferences of either parent. But Fatima's community—her mosque, her family, her social network—told her that a civil divorce was not a real divorce; that without a *talaq* from her husband, she would remain married in Allah's eyes and would be committing adultery if she remarried; and that she should submit the matter to the mosque's dispute resolution panel, which would apply Islamic principles to reach a settlement.

The panel applied classical sharia. The outcome reflected classical sharia's provisions on divorce, custody, and property—provisions that give the husband significant advantages over the wife in all three areas. Fatima accepted the outcome not because she freely chose it but because the social and religious pressure was overwhelming and because she did not fully understand that she had another option.

Fatima's story is not unique. It is echoed in the experiences of Muslim women across the United States who find themselves effectively operating under a parallel legal system that their community enforces through social pressure, religious authority, and the genuine fear—instilled by Islamic dogma—that defying the community's religious structures will have consequences not just in this life but in the next.

The Fourteenth Amendment's equal protection guarantee applies to

Fatima. The constitutional right to a fair family court proceeding applies to Fatima. The civil rights that American law has painstakingly constructed to protect women in divorce and custody proceedings apply to Fatima. But those rights are effectively nullified when a parallel legal system—operating outside civil courts but with sufficient community authority to coerce compliance—applies rules that contradict or suppress the opportunity to claim them.

THE NON-MUSLIM IN THE SHARIA NEIGHBORHOOD

The problem extends beyond Muslim women. It extends to non-Muslims who find themselves living adjacent to, doing business with, or in legal disputes with members of communities where sharia norms are applied with something *approaching* institutional force.

In several American cities, there are already neighborhoods and communities where the cultural and institutional influence of Islamist organizations is strong enough that non-Muslims experience a de facto pressure to conform to Islamic norms—in commercial dealings, in community relations, and in the implicit expectations about acceptable behavior. This pressure is not *yet* a legal problem in most cases. It is a social and cultural one. But it represents the early stages of exactly the kind of parallel jurisdiction that, if given formal legal recognition, would eventually produce the *dhimmi* dynamic that Chapter Four described: non-Muslims navigating a social and institutional environment governed by rules that assign them lower status than their Muslim neighbors.

The dhimmi system, remember, is not merely a medieval historical curiosity. It is the classical sharia framework for governing non-Muslims—a framework that prescribes their legal subordination, limits their religious expression, extracts special obligations from them, and makes their legal standing in disputes with Muslims structurally inferior. When Islamist organizations in the United States argue for sharia accommodation—for recognition of sharia arbitration, for sharia-compatible regulations in public institutions, for the application of Islamic standards in disputes involving Muslims—the framework they ask the courts to honor is the classical one documented in Chapter Four—one that assigns non-Muslims a subordinate legal status. That consequence follows from the content of the framework itself, regardless of any individual advocate's stated intentions.

Far from a paranoid projection, such realities are the logical and natural consequences of a legal system whose classical form explicitly assigns different legal rights to different people based on their religion. You cannot partially import sharia's legal framework without importing its inherent hierarchical structure. The hierarchy is not a bug in the system. It *is* the system.

WHAT COURTS HAVE SAID

American courts have not been uniformly naïve about sharia's incompatibility with constitutional principles. Several state courts have refused to enforce sharia arbitration outcomes that violate constitutional rights, and their reasoning is instructive.

In *Jabri v. Qaddura* (Texas, 2003), a Texas appellate court refused to enforce a sharia arbitration agreement in a family law case, noting that the agreement did not meet the requirements for binding arbitration under Texas law and that the substantive outcomes it produced were inconsistent with Texas family law's protections.

In *Hosain v. Malik* (Maryland, 1996), a Maryland court was asked to enforce a Pakistani custody order that had been issued under Islamic law. The court refused, finding that the Pakistani court's application of Islamic custody principles—which presumptively favor the father over the mother after a certain age—did not comport with the best interests of the child standard that Maryland law requires.

In New Jersey, in *S.D. v. M.J.R.* (2010), a trial court judge initially refused to issue a restraining order against a Muslim husband who had repeatedly raped his wife, ruling that because the husband believed Islamic law permitted him to have sexual relations with his wife without her consent, he lacked the criminal intent required for the offense. The appellate court reversed this decision swiftly and decisively, ruling that the husband's religious beliefs did not exempt him from New Jersey's domestic violence law. But the trial court's initial ruling—its willingness to treat Islamic law as a valid defense against a criminal charge—illustrates well the danger that arises when sharia principles are given even informal legal weight.

That New Jersey trial court's initial decision is a warning in judicial form.

It shows what happens when a judge, in possibly well-intentioned multicultural sensitivity, begins to treat a religious legal system as a legitimate framework for evaluating conduct that civil law clearly prohibits. The appellate court corrected the error—that time. But the pressure to accommodate, to defer, to treat sharia as a legitimate parallel legal authority, is persistent and will produce more such errors unless Americans understand clearly why accommodation is constitutionally impermissible.

THE VOLUNTARINESS PROBLEM

The standard defense of sharia arbitration in the United States is that it is entirely voluntary—that no one is compelled to submit to Islamic dispute resolution, and that the constitutional problems therefore do not arise. If both parties freely choose sharia arbitration, the argument goes, there is no constitutional violation. They have simply exercised their private autonomy.

This argument has surface plausibility—and frequently fails in practice.

Voluntariness, in the legal sense that matters for enforceable arbitration, requires that both parties enter the agreement freely and with genuine understanding of their alternatives. It requires informed consent—that a woman who submits a divorce dispute to a sharia council knows that civil courts offer her legally enforceable remedies independent of her husband's religious consent, and that she is not misled about the binding nature or legal consequences of the religious proceeding. This is the standard that contract and arbitration law demands, and it is the standard that sharia arbitration proceedings have sometimes failed to meet—not because religious communities have no right to their own norms and expectations, but because an agreement reached through misinformation or without genuine understanding of available alternatives is not a freely made choice in any sense that the law should recognize.

It should be said plainly: religious communities have every right to maintain their own standards and to respond when members choose civil processes over religious ones. A mosque may counsel its members. A community may express disapproval. These are legitimate exercises of religious and associational freedom that the Constitution protects. The legal concern is narrower and more specific: whether the arbitration agreement itself was genuinely informed and freely made—and whether civil courts, in enforcing its outcomes, are giving legal force to a process that stripped one party of rights the Constitution guarantees.

The voluntariness defense serves Islamist organizations well because it frames a constitutional objection as a civil rights complaint. It is a sophisticated legal strategy, not a sincere commitment to free choice.

THE CONSTITUTIONAL LINE

The Constitution draws a clear line—not always a simple one to locate in specific cases, but clear in principle—between what religious accommodation requires and what it prohibits.

It requires protecting every individual's right to practice his or her faith privately and freely. It requires permitting voluntary religious arbitration between consenting parties who understand their alternatives and are not coerced. It requires allowing religious communities to govern their internal affairs through their own processes, as long as those processes do not violate the constitutional rights of their members.

It prohibits enforcing the outcomes of religious arbitration when those outcomes violate constitutional rights. It prohibits allowing a religious legal system to function as a parallel jurisdiction with coercive authority over community members who have not genuinely and freely consented. It prohibits applying religious legal standards in civil courts in ways that produce unequal treatment of parties based on their religion, gender, or any other constitutionally protected characteristic. And it prohibits, absolutely, the recognition of any system—religious or otherwise—that assigns different legal rights to different people based on their faith.

Classical sharia, in its treatment of women, of non-Muslims, of apostates, of those accused of blasphemy, and of anyone who invokes rights that sharia does not recognize, produces outcomes that violate every one of these prohibitions—not in some interpretations, nor in extreme applications, but in its classical, authoritative form, as derived from the Quran, the hadith, and the accumulated rulings of Islamic jurisprudence—the very form that Islamist organizations cite as the basis for their advocacy.

A legal system in which your rights depend on which community's law governs your dispute is not a variation of the American constitutional tradition. It is its antithesis—the feudal, sectarian world the Constitution was designed to replace. It is the feudal, sectarian, hierarchical world that the

Constitution was designed to replace: a world in which Christians had different rights than Jews, men had different rights than women, and the powerful defined the law for the powerless in the name of God.

America replaced that world with something intentional: something imperfect, perpetually argued over, and still being improved—but built on the foundational commitment that the law belongs to everyone equally. That commitment is not a Western cultural preference. It is the hard-won achievement of people who understood, from experience, what life looks like when the law plays favorites.

WHAT THE ISLAMIST STRATEGY DEPENDS ON

The advance of sharia-compatible norms in American law and institutions will depend, at every stage, on Americans failing to make a crucial distinction—the distinction between protecting Muslim Americans' right to practice their faith, on the one hand, and accommodating a political-legal system that subordinates other Americans on the basis of their religion, on the other.

Islamist advocacy organizations are sophisticated. They know that the word *sharia* has become radioactive in American public discourse, so they increasingly avoid it, cloaking their advocacy in the language of religious accommodation, cultural sensitivity, and civil rights. They weaponize buzzwords like 'bigotry' and 'Islamophobia.' They argue that any resistance to sharia arbitration recognition is discrimination against Muslims. They insist that any examination of classical sharia's legal hierarchies is 'Islamophobic.' They argue that the constitutional protections for religious freedom require the state to defer to Islamic legal standards in disputes involving Muslim parties.

Each of these arguments is crafted to make Americans feel that constitutional principle *requires* accommodation—when in fact constitutional principle requires exactly the opposite. The First Amendment's Free Exercise Clause does not require the state to enforce the outcomes of a legal system that violates the Fourteenth Amendment's equal protection guarantee. Religious freedom does not include the freedom to subject other people—such as women or non-Muslims—to a legal framework that assigns them inferior rights. The Constitution's protection of religious practice does not extend to the protection of religious governance.

Understanding these distinctions is not 'Islamophobia'—which is largely a constructed term used to shield Islamic teachings from evaluation and critical assessment. This understanding is constitutional literacy—and it is precisely the form of literacy that Islamist organizations have the most to lose from Americans acquiring.

CONCLUSION: ONE LAW, INDIVISIBLE

America is a country of extraordinary religious diversity. Its history is, among other things, the history of one religious community after another finding its place in the constitutional framework—learning that its faith can flourish precisely because the law did not favor it or persecute it, but simply left it free to be practiced in peace while holding everyone, believer and unbeliever alike, to the same civil standards.

That history has required, from every community that has participated in it, a particular act of civic maturity: the recognition that your religious law governs your personal life, not your unconsenting neighbors' lives, and that the civil law that governs everyone must be kept separate from the religious law that governs you. Catholic Americans accept that the Church's prohibition on divorce does not mean that civil divorce is unavailable to their non-Catholic neighbors. Jewish Americans accept that *halakha*'s dietary laws do not govern what their gentile neighbors may eat. Protestant Americans accept that their understanding of biblical law does not give them the right to impose its standards on citizens who do not share their faith.

This civic maturity—this willingness to keep religious law in its proper sphere while participating in a shared civil order built on equal protection and popular sovereignty—is what every religious community in America has been asked to demonstrate. And it is what classical sharia, in its authoritative form, explicitly refuses to provide. This is not a statement about Muslim Americans, millions of whom are good citizens whose faith coexists fully with constitutional citizenship. It is a statement about classical sharia as a political-legal system, which claims a universal jurisdiction that does not respect the boundary between religious practice and civil governance. It claims the right to govern not just the believer's personal life but the life of every person in its reach—including the non-Muslim, the woman seeking equal rights, the homosexual practitioner whose behavior it condemns, and the apostate whose departure it punishes with death.

That claim is incompatible with one law for all. It is incompatible with equal protection. It is incompatible with the constitutional order that protects every American—including every Muslim American—from the imposition of any other community's religious law.

One law. By the people. For all. Without exception, without parallel, and without apology. That is not a threat to Muslim Americans. It is their protection—the same protection provided to every American of every faith.

It is the Constitution doing exactly what it was designed to do.

8

CONCLUSION: THE CONSTITUTION IS NOT NEUTRAL ABOUT ITS OWN DESTRUCTION—A CALL TO CLARITY, COURAGE, AND CONSTITUTIONAL DEFENSE

There is a question that every generation of Americans has had to answer for itself in the real circumstances of their own time, with their own country's future hanging in the balance. The question is this: Are we willing to defend what we have built or inherited, not with weapons, nor with hostility toward our neighbors, but with something that has proven, across the long arc of American history, to be just as essential as any army: clarity? Are we willing to see clearly, speak plainly, and act on what we know to be true—even when powerful forces insist that seeing clearly is bigotry, speaking plainly is hatred, and acting on truth is discrimination?

This book has been an exercise in clarity, an honest examination of a political-legal system—classical sharia, in its authoritative form, as derived from the Quran, the hadith, and the accumulated jurisprudence of fourteen centuries of Islamic legal scholarship—and a sober assessment of whether that system is compatible with the United States Constitution.

The answer, demonstrated chapter by chapter, is no. Not in some interpretations. Not in extreme applications. Not because of cultural misunderstanding or political prejudice. But because the primary sources of classical sharia—the very sources that Islamist movements cite as their authority—establish legal hierarchies, political doctrines, and criminal penalties that contradict the Constitution's core principles at every point of contact.

WHAT THIS BOOK HAS SHOWN

Let us state the argument plainly one final time, because clarity requires not just assertion but demonstration—and the demonstration has been made.

Chapter One showed that sharia's foundational doctrine of *hakimiyya*—divine sovereignty—is a direct challenge to the First Amendment's Establishment Clause. Sharia does not seek merely to coexist alongside the Constitution. It claims that the Constitution, as a man-made document, possesses no legitimate authority before Allah's revealed law. That claim is not a fringe interpretation. It is the constitutional premise of classical Islamic political theology, derived from Quranic verses that Islamic jurists have consistently interpreted for fourteen centuries. A legal system that regards the Constitution as an illegitimate usurpation of divine sovereignty cannot be accommodated within a constitutional order without that order eventually yielding.

Chapter Two demonstrated that apostasy law—the death penalty for leaving Islam, grounded in Muhammad's explicit command that "whoever changes his Islamic religion, kill him"—is an irreconcilable contradiction of the First Amendment's guarantee of religious freedom. The freedom to leave a faith is the most basic expression of religious liberty. A legal system that prescribes death for exercising that freedom is not a different approach to religion. It is the abolition of religious freedom, enforced by the threat of execution.

Chapter Three explained that sharia's blasphemy doctrine—derived from Muhammad's personal ordering of assassinations for those who criticized him, systematized by Ibn Taymiyya and Ibn Qayyim into a comprehensive legal mandate for killing those who insult the Prophet—is the First Amendment's direct antithesis. Free speech means nothing if the speech that matters most—criticism of the powerful, challenge to the sacred, questioning of what authorities demand we accept—can be silenced by the threat of death. From the killing of Ka'b ibn al-Ashraf in seventh-century Medina to the beheading of Samuel Paty on a French street in 2020, the doctrine has demonstrated its lethal consistency across fourteen centuries.

Chapter Four explained that sharia's legal hierarchy—with Muslim men at the apex, Muslim women subordinated by Quranic command, and Christians and Jews assigned permanent *dhimmi* status, paying the *jizya* "while feeling themselves subdued," their testimony discounted in court, their blood money set at half the value of a Muslim's, their churches prohibited from being built or repaired—is a comprehensive violation of the Fourteenth Amendment's equal protection guarantee. The dhimmi system is not an historical artifact. It is classical sharia's governing framework for non-Muslims—and it is what Islamist movements seek to restore.

Chapter Five showed that the *hudud* punishments—amputation for theft, public flogging for alcohol and extramarital sex, stoning to death for adultery, death for homosexuality—are not merely inconsistent with the Eighth Amendment's prohibition on cruel and unusual punishment. They are its categorical opposite: punishments derived from divine command, immune to human evaluation or reform, designed to inflict suffering as an expression of Allah's authority, and applied in the twenty-first century in Saudi Arabia, Iran, Afghanistan, and wherever classical sharia governs. People who engage in homosexual acts, under classical sharia, are not second-class citizens. They are despised and condemned to death—by hadith, by jurisprudential consensus, and by the practice of every state that applies classical Islamic criminal law.

Chapter Six emphasized that sharia's doctrine of divine sovereignty—its location of ultimate political authority in Allah rather than in the consent of the governed—is incompatible with the constitutional foundation of popular sovereignty. Democracy, in classical Islamic political theology, is not a different form of government. It is a form of infidelity and idolatry—the substitution of human judgment for divine command. The Islamist project, whether expressed through the Muslim Brotherhood's patient long-term strategy or through ISIS's brutal short-term caliphate, is not a movement seeking a seat at democracy's table. It is a movement seeking to replace the table with a throne.

Chapter Seven showed that the push for sharia arbitration recognition in American courts—framed as religious accommodation, driven by sophisticated legal advocacy, documented in Britain's lamentable cautionary experience—is the institutional mechanism through which a parallel legal order is advanced. That order subordinates women, excludes non-Muslims from equal legal standing, and operates through community coercion that renders the fiction of voluntariness practically meaningless for those with the least power. One law for all is not a slogan. It is the constitutional principle on which every American's rights depend—and it is the principle that parallel sharia jurisdiction directly threatens.

THE SOURCES SPEAK FOR THEMSELVES

Throughout this book, the argument has rested on primary sources—the Quran, the authenticated hadith, the rulings of the classical jurists. This basis is deliberate and it is essential.

The case against sharia's compatibility with the Constitution does not rest on what critics say about Islam. It rests on what Islam's own most authoritative texts—deemed "sacred" by the masses—say about itself. The Quran's command that judgment belongs only to Allah. Muhammad's command that the apostate be killed. Ibn Taymiyya's legal mandate that the blasphemer be executed without the possibility of reprieve. The juristic prescription that the dhimmi's blood money be half that of a Muslim. The hadith's command that those who do as Lot's people did be killed. These principles are not Western misreadings of Islamic sources. They are Islamic sources, read as Islamic scholars have always read them.

This fact matters enormously because the primary strategy of Islamist advocacy in Western countries is to shift the discussion away from the content of the sources and toward the motivations of the critics. Critics are accused of 'Islamophobia,' their credentials are questioned, or they are dismissed as lacking knowledge of Arabic. They are asked to produce a Muslim scholar who supports their interpretation. The focus moves from what the Islamic texts say to the alleged prejudices of the critic. So long as the discussion centers on the critic, it does not address the Quran, Muhammad's model of conduct, or what primary Muslim sources reveal. And as long as Americans are exerting energy defending themselves against charges of bigotry, they are not examining those primary sources.

This book has examined the primary sources. The sources speak for themselves. And what they say—clearly, consistently, across fourteen centuries of legal development—is that classical sharia establishes a political-legal order that cannot coexist with the constitutional principles of the United States. Not because the Constitution is hostile to religion. But because classical sharia is, in its own explicit terms, hostile to the constitutional order.

WHAT CONGRESS HAS RECOGNIZED

This analysis is not the idiosyncratic conclusion of one scholar working in isolation. It has been affirmed in the most consequential deliberative body in the United States.

Congressional hearings on the threat of political Islam and sharia to the American constitutional order have been held over multiple legislative sessions, with testimony from national security experts, constitutional scholars, former Muslims, and survivors of sharia governance. Those hearings have documented the organizational infrastructure of Islamist movements in the United States—the funding from Gulf states, the penetration of academic institutions, the strategic use of civil rights language to advance sharia-compatible norms, the documented connections between ostensibly moderate advocacy organizations and the Muslim Brotherhood's global network.

The congressional record makes clear what this book has argued from its first page: the concern about sharia is not a concern about Muslim individuals practicing their faith. It is a concern about a well-funded, strategically sophisticated political movement—known as political Islam or Islamism—that is using every tool that American democracy provides to advance a legal and political framework that would ultimately destroy the freedoms upon which those tools depend.

This topic is a matter of constitutional defense. The men and women in Congress who have raised these concerns are not engaged in religious discrimination. They are doing what elected representatives in a constitutional democracy are obligated to do: defend the Constitution against threats that originate not from foreign armies but from ideological movements that operate from within, using the language of rights to erode the foundations on which rights rest.

THE MUSLIMS WHO AGREE

Before this conclusion goes further, something must be said that is easily forgotten in the heat of this debate: there are Muslims—many Muslims—who share the concerns expressed in this book. They are often known as modernist, progressive, or liberal Muslims.

Former Muslims who have left Islam and built new lives in the freedom that America provides. Muslim reformers who argue that Islamic political theology must be honestly confronted and genuinely reformed if Muslim communities are to thrive in democratic societies. Muslim women who have experienced sharia's legal hierarchies firsthand and who came to America specifically because they wanted to live under a different law. Muslim men and women who practice their faith privately and peacefully and who are themselves threatened by the Islamist movements that claim to speak for all Muslims while advancing an agenda that most individual Muslims never voted for and many actively oppose.

These voices exist. They are brave. They are often threatened—by the same Islamist organizations that threaten everyone else who challenges sharia's authority. They deserve to be heard, supported, and protected. And their existence is the most powerful demonstration that opposing Islamism is not opposing Muslims.

When a Saudi-born American woman says that sharia's treatment of women is incompatible with the Constitution, she is not expressing anti-Muslim bigotry. She is expressing the hard-won wisdom of someone who has lived on both sides of the line. When an Egyptian Christian who fled his country says that the dhimmi system is alive and functioning in the Middle East, he is not trafficking in prejudice. He is reporting from experience. When a Pakistani former Muslim says that blasphemy laws destroyed families he knew, he is not inventing a problem. He is bearing witness to a reality that comfortable Western academics have the luxury of theorizing away.

Their testimony is part of this book's foundation, even where it is not quoted directly. And their courage in speaking when Islamist organizations work hard to silence them is an example that all Americans who value the truth should honor.

WHAT IS AT STAKE

Americans sometimes speak of defending democracy as if it were a rhetorical abstraction—a phrase for speeches and textbooks, something that exists independently of the choices that ordinary citizens make in ordinary moments. It is not. Democracy is a constant exercise and daily achievement. It requires, from its citizens, the consistent exercise of the civic virtues that sustain it: the willingness to be informed, to speak honestly, to resist the comfortable lie, and to defend the principles of the constitutional order even when—especially when—defending them is socially costly.

What is at stake in the debate over sharia and the Constitution is not a policy disagreement about immigration levels or foreign policy priorities. It is a question about the nature of the American republic itself. It is the question of whether this country will maintain the constitutional principles that protect every citizen—Muslim, Christian, Jewish, secular, and everything in between—from the imposition of any community's religious law, or whether —through a combination of willful ignorance, religious intimidation, political cowardice, and the systematic exploitation of American tolerance by organizations that do not share it—those principles will be slowly eroded until the foundation they rest on is too weakened to support them.

The erosion does not happen all at once. It happens the way all erosion happens—gradually, incrementally, through a thousand small concessions that each seem reasonable in isolation and are catastrophic in aggregate. A university that stops inviting speakers who criticize Islamic law. A court that applies Islamic standards to a family dispute. A legislature that passes a resolution condemning 'Islamophobia' without defining the term, thereby making honest analysis of Islamic doctrine politically dangerous. A textbook that describes sharia as a personal spiritual code without mentioning its political-legal dimensions, or its harms to minorities and non-Muslims. A journalist who self-censors rather than report what the primary sources actually say. Each concession is small. Together, they constitute the surrender of the intellectual and institutional ground on which constitutional defense depends.

The First Amendment cannot protect itself. The Fourteenth Amendment cannot enforce itself. The separation of church and state does not maintain itself. These constitutional principles require citizens who understand them, believe in them, and are willing to defend them—not with hatred, not with violence, not with discrimination against Muslim Americans who are themselves protected by the same principles—but with the clear-eyed, well-informed, morally serious commitment to constitutional truth that is the only adequate response to a sophisticated ideological challenge.

WHAT YOU OWE YOUR COUNTRY

If you have read this book and found its arguments persuasive, the question that follows is: what do you do with what you now know?

The answer is not to fear your Muslim neighbors. It is not to view every mosque as a threat or every Muslim as an Islamist. It is not to abandon the American commitment to religious freedom that protects Muslim Americans alongside everyone else. These responses would be wrong, they would be unjust, and they would, ironically, undermine the constitutional principles this book exists to defend.

The answer is to be informed and to inform others. To understand the distinction—the critical, foundational distinction—between Islam as a personal faith practiced by millions of peaceful, decent people, and Islamism as a political movement advancing a legal system incompatible with constitutional government. To make that distinction clearly and refuse to surrender it under pressure. To call out the Islamist advocacy organizations that exploit American tolerance while working to undermine it. To support Muslim reformers who are fighting, at great personal risk, for a version of their faith that can genuinely coexist with constitutional democracy. To demand from your elected representatives the clarity and courage that this issue requires.

To read the primary sources. To ask the hard questions. To refuse the comfortable silence that Islamist organizations depend on to advance their agenda unchallenged.

And to remember, always, what you are defending—not a culture, not a majority religion, not a particular political party, but a set of constitutional principles that belong to every American equally. The First Amendment that protects Muslim prayer also protects the criticism of Muhammad. The Fourteenth Amendment that protects Muslims' equal legal standing also protects the Christian 'dhimmi' from second-class legal status. The Eighth Amendment that protects Muslim defendants from cruel punishment also protects the homosexual American from the death penalty that classical sharia prescribes for his behavior. These principles are indivisible. They stand together or they fall together. And they will stand only as long as Americans are willing to understand them clearly enough to defend them honestly.

THE CONSTITUTION'S FINAL ANSWER

The United States Constitution is not a neutral document. It does not take a neutral position on slavery—it eventually abolished it. It does not take a neutral position on the denial of women's suffrage—it eventually corrected it. It does not take a neutral position on racial segregation—it eventually prohibited it. And it does not take a neutral position on legal systems that assign different rights to different human beings based on their religion, prescribe death for changing your faith or criticizing a so-called prophet, mandate the amputation of hands and the stoning of adulterers, and locate ultimate sovereignty in Allah rather than in the consent of the governed.

On all of these questions, the Constitution has good and clear answers. They are not perfect answers—no human document is perfect. But they are answers grounded in the hard-won wisdom of people who understood, from experience, what the alternatives look like. They are answers that have been tested and refined through the bloodiest conflicts and the most consequential legal struggles in American history. And they are answers that point, consistently and unmistakably, away from theocracy and toward liberty—away from legal hierarchy and toward equal protection—away from divine sovereignty imposed by jurists and toward popular sovereignty exercised by free citizens.

Classical sharia points in the exact opposite direction. Not incidentally. Not in some interpretations. In its primary sources, in its authoritative jurisprudence, in the explicit goals of the Islamist movements that promote it—sharia points toward theocracy, legal hierarchy, divine sovereignty, and the permanent subordination of those who do not submit to its authority.

America has built something worth defending. Something that took centuries of struggle, oceans of sacrifice, and the hard work of generation after generation of citizens who believed that human beings could govern themselves and protect each other's rights without a divine mandate telling them how. Something imperfect and perpetually unfinished but grounded in the most liberating political idea ever in human history: that the people are sovereign, that every person is equal before the law, and that no deity, no prophet, no jurist, and no self-appointed spokesman for divine will has the right to override that sovereignty.

That idea is under challenge. The challenge is vicious, sophisticated, patient, and well-funded. It wears the language of civil rights and speaks the vocabulary of tolerance. It exploits the genuine American commitment to religious freedom to advance a system that would ultimately abolish religious freedom for everyone who does not submit to its authority.

This challenge must be named. It must be understood. It must be opposed—not with fear, not with violence, not with hatred, but with the full force of constitutional clarity and civic courage.

We the People built this republic. We the People must defend it. The Constitution is counting on us. So is every American—of every faith, of every background, of every generation yet to come—whose freedom depends on our courage to defend it.

Here we stand; we can do no other.

APPENDIX: SHARIA PRINCIPLES IN CONFLICT WITH THE U.S. CONSTITUTION

A Reference Guide for American Readers

The following is a concise, direct reference list of classical sharia principles —stated in their original Arabic, transliterated for English readers, and translated plainly—alongside the specific provisions of the United States Constitution they contradict. These rulings are not obscure or disputed. Each principle listed here reflects the mainstream, authoritative position of classical Islamic jurisprudence, derived from the Quran, the authenticated hadith, and the accumulated rulings of the major schools of Islamic *fiqh*. They are the rulings that Islamist movements cite as their authority and that Islamic states apply as their law.

This appendix is designed as a quick-reference tool—a document that any American citizen, legislator, educator, or concerned reader can consult to see, at a glance, exactly where classical sharia and the Constitution come into irreconcilable conflict. The chapters of this book have examined each conflict in depth. This appendix states them plainly, without elaboration, so that the incompatibility is impossible to overlook or explain away.

The Arabic is provided not as decoration but as documentation. These terms are the actual words of the legal tradition—words that have governed the lives of millions of people across fourteen centuries and that Islamist organizations advancing sharia in America cite in their own internal communications and religious rulings. Americans deserve to know them.

I.

لَا وِلَايَةَ لِغَيْرِ الْمُسْلِمِ عَلَى الْمُسْلِمِ

Lā wilāya li-ghayr al-Muslim ʿalā al-Muslim: **"A non-Muslim has no authority over a Muslim."**

This principle is one of the most foundational rules of classical Islamic governance. *Wilaya*—authority, guardianship, rulership—is categorically denied to non-Muslims in any position that would place them in a superior role over Muslims, whether in judicial, governmental, military, or administrative contexts. A Christian cannot be a judge in a sharia court. A Jew cannot hold a position of political authority over a Muslim population. A non-Muslim cannot, under classical sharia, be a head of state, a military commander, or a court official in any capacity that grants him authority over Muslim subjects. This injunction is not an incidental rule but a structural principle of Islamic governance—one that flows directly from the theological premise that Islam is the supreme religion and that its adherents are the superior legal class.

Constitutional conflicts:

Article VI, Clause 3—"No religious test shall ever be required as a qualification to any office or public trust under the United States." The Constitution categorically prohibits the exclusion of any person from public office based on religion. Classical sharia categorically requires it.

Fourteenth Amendment—Equal citizenship regardless of religion. Sharia's permanent prohibition on non-Muslim authority over Muslims creates a two-tiered citizenship in which non-Muslims are constitutionally ineligible for positions of authority—a direct violation of equal protection.

2.

مَنْ بَدَّلَ دِينَهُ فَاقْتُلُوهُ

Man baddala dīnahu fa-qtulūhu: **"Whoever changes his religion, kill him."**

This quotation is Muhammad's direct command regarding apostasy, recorded in *Sahih al-Bukhari*—the most authoritative hadith collection in Sunni Islam—and is accepted as authentic and legally binding by every major classical school of Islamic jurisprudence. The ruling requires no judicial elaboration: a Muslim who leaves Islam forfeits his right to live. The classical schools prescribe a waiting period during which the apostate is urged to recant, but if he refuses, the sentence is death. The ruling applies to any form of leaving Islam—converting to Christianity, Judaism, or any other religion; embracing atheism; or publicly rejecting Islamic doctrine. It is enforced as law today in Saudi Arabia, Iran, Afghanistan, and other countries governed by classical sharia.

Constitutional conflicts:

First Amendment, Free Exercise Clause—The Constitution absolutely protects every person's right to practice, change, or abandon any religion without government interference or penalty. The freedom to leave a faith is the most basic expression of religious liberty. A legal system that prescribes death for exercising that freedom is not a different approach to religion—it is the abolition of religious freedom enforced by execution.

Eighth Amendment—The death penalty for the non-violent act of changing one's religious belief constitutes cruel and unusual punishment by any standard recognized by American constitutional law.

3.

دِينُ الدَّوْلَةِ الإِسْلَامُ

Dīn al-dawla al-Islām: **"The religion of the state is Islam."**

This principle—enshrined in the constitutions of Egypt, Saudi Arabia, Pakistan, Afghanistan, Iran, and dozens of other Muslim-majority states—reflects the classical Islamic conviction that the state is not a neutral arbiter of competing interests but an instrument for the implementation and protection of Islamic law. The Islamic state's purpose is not to protect the rights of all citizens equally but to fulfill God's command by governing according to sharia. Non-Muslims are tolerated conditionally—as *dhimmis*, under the rules examined throughout this book—but the state's fundamental identity and legal authority are Islamic. This designation is not a cultural preference or a ceremonial acknowledgment of majority religion. It is a constitutional principle with direct legal consequences for every non-Muslim citizen.

Constitutional conflict:

First Amendment, Establishment Clause—"Congress shall make no law respecting an establishment of religion." The Establishment Clause prohibits the United States government—at every level—from designating any religion as the religion of the state. The principle that the state's religion is Islam is the precise arrangement that the Establishment Clause was designed to prevent, applied to a different religion but identical in structure.

4.

الْجِزْيَةُ عَلَى أَهْلِ الذِّمَّةِ

Al-jizya ʿalā ahl al-dhimma: **"The *jizya* tax is imposed on non-Muslim subjects."**

The *jizya* is the poll tax that classical sharia levies on Christians and Jews living under Islamic governance as a condition of their toleration. It is prescribed in Quran 9:29, which commands that it be collected until the non-Muslim "feels himself subdued." Classical commentators—including Ibn Kathir, the most widely read Quranic commentator in the Sunni world—specify that the manner of collection must be humiliating: the dhimmi pays standing while the Muslim collector sits; the act of payment is an embodied acknowledgment of Islamic supremacy and non-Muslim subordination. The *jizya* is not a neutral revenue measure. It is a performative instrument of legal degradation—a regular, institutionalized reminder that the non-Muslim's continued existence in Islamic society is conditional on his submission and his payment.

Constitutional conflicts:

Fourteenth Amendment, Equal Protection Clause—No state shall deny to any person equal protection of the laws. A tax levied exclusively on citizens of a specific religion—as a marker of their inferior legal status and as a condition of their toleration—is a textbook violation of equal protection. The Constitution knows no class of citizens who must pay for the right to exist in their own country.

General constitutional principle of equal taxation—The Constitution's framework of equal citizenship prohibits the government from imposing differential financial burdens on citizens based on their religion.

5.

شَهَادَةُ الْمَرْأَةِ نِصْفُ شَهَادَةِ الرَّجُلِ

Shahādat al-mar'a niṣf shahādat al-rajul: **"A woman's testimony is worth half that of a man's."**

This ruling derives directly from the Quran (Surah 2:282), which instructs that in financial transactions, two women should substitute for one male witness "in case one of them errs, the other can remind her." Muhammad confirmed the principle in the hadith recorded in *Sahih al-Bukhari*, explaining that women are "deficient in reason," as evidenced by the fact that their testimony carries half the legal weight of a man's. Classical jurisprudence extended this principle across legal categories: in criminal cases involving the *hudud* penalties, women's testimony is inadmissible altogether in several schools; in civil and financial matters, the two-for-one rule applies. The result is a courtroom in which a woman's account of what she witnessed, experienced, or suffered carries systematically less legal weight than any man's—not because of the credibility of her specific testimony, but because of her sex.

Constitutional conflict:

Fourteenth Amendment, Equal Protection Clause—The Supreme Court has consistently held that sex-based legal classifications must survive heightened scrutiny and cannot rest on outdated stereotypes about women's capacities. A rule assigning women categorically half the testimonial weight of men—grounded explicitly in the claim that women are intellectually deficient—cannot survive even the most deferential constitutional review.

6.

لِلذَّكَرِ مِثْلُ حَظِّ الْأُنْثَيَيْنِ

Li-l-dhakari mithlu ḥaẓẓ al-unthayayn: **"A male receives the share of two females."**

This decree is a direct Quranic ruling on inheritance, stated explicitly in Surah 4:11: "Allah instructs you concerning your children: for the male, what is equal to the share of two females." The rule applies across the inheritance structure—a son inherits twice what a daughter inherits, a brother twice what a sister inherits, a husband twice what a wife inherits in the same circumstances. Islamic jurists regard this ruling as among the most clearly established in all of sharia, derived directly from explicit Quranic command and therefore beyond legislative revision. The classical justification—that men bear greater financial obligations in Islamic society, including the *mahr* and the maintenance of the family—does not change the fact that the rule assigns different legal entitlements to men and women as a matter of divine prescription.

Constitutional conflict:

Fourteenth Amendment, Equal Protection Clause—The Supreme Court has held that laws treating men and women differently with respect to property rights and inheritance are subject to heightened constitutional scrutiny and are generally impermissible. A rule assigning women half the inheritance of men as a categorical, religion-based legal command cannot be enforced in American courts without violating equal protection.

7.

حَدُّ السَّرِقَةِ قَطْعُ الْيَدِ

Ḥadd al-sariqa qaṭʿ al-yad: **"The prescribed punishment for theft is cutting off the hand."**

This *hadd* penalty is prescribed directly in the Quran, Surah 5:38: "As for the thief, the male and the female, cut off their hands as punishment for what they committed as a deterrent from Allah." It is applied as law in Saudi Arabia, Iran, Sudan, Afghanistan under the Taliban, and in the territories formerly controlled by ISIS. The amputation is of the right hand at the wrist, performed judicially, for theft meeting the classical conditions of the *nisab* (minimum value) and *hirz* (secured location). The punishment is permanent, irreversible, and publicly visible—designed not merely to penalize the offender but to mark his body permanently as a deterrent to others and as an expression of God's authority over human conduct.

Constitutional conflict:

Eighth Amendment—The prohibition on cruel and unusual punishment applies categorically to judicial mutilation. No American court has ever upheld the amputation of a body part as a criminal penalty, and no Eighth Amendment analysis—under any standard the Supreme Court has articulated—could sustain such a punishment. The permanent, irreversible destruction of a healthy body part as a criminal sentence is cruel and unusual by every measure of evolving standards of decency that the Court has applied.

8.

حَدُّ الزِّنَا الرَّجْمُ لِلْمُحْصَنِ

Ḥadd al-zinā al-rajm li-l-muḥṣan: **"The prescribed punishment for adultery by a married person is stoning to death."**

This hadd penalty is grounded in the authenticated hadith—Muhammad personally ordered and supervised stonings for adultery, as documented in *Sahih al-Bukhari* and *Sahih Muslim*—and is the unanimous ruling of all four major Sunni schools of jurisprudence. The condemned person is partially buried before the stoning begins, stones of a prescribed size are used, and the execution is communal—members of the public participate in throwing the stones, making the entire community complicit in the enforcement of divine law. The punishment is applied today in Iran, Saudi Arabia, Afghanistan, and parts of Nigeria. It is among the most unambiguously documented hudud penalties in the classical tradition.

Constitutional conflicts:

Eighth Amendment—Stoning to death is among the most prolonged, painful, and deliberately agonizing forms of execution in the historical record. It constitutes cruel and unusual punishment in the most categorical sense—a method of killing designed to maximize suffering as an expression of divine authority, with no penological justification that American constitutional law would recognize.

Fourteenth Amendment—The Supreme Court has recognized, in its substantive due process jurisprudence, liberty interests in personal and intimate conduct. The state's imposition of death for consensual adult conduct in the private sphere violates those liberty interests completely.

9.

وُجُوبُ طَاعَةِ وَلِيِّ الْأَمْرِ

Wujūb ṭāʿat walī al-amr: **"Obedience to the ruler is obligatory."**

This principle—derived from Quran 4:59 ("Obey Allah and obey the Messenger and those in authority among you") and elaborated extensively in classical Islamic political theology—establishes a duty of political obedience that flows from divine command rather than from popular consent or constitutional structure. The ruler (*walī al-amr*) derives his authority from his role as guardian of Islamic law, and obedience to him is framed as an extension of obedience to God. Dissent, in this framework, is not a protected right but a potential act of rebellion against divine order. Classical Islamic political thought made limited allowance for disobedience only when the ruler commanded something explicitly forbidden by sharia—but even then, the mechanisms for legitimate political opposition bore no resemblance to the constitutional structures of democratic accountability.

Constitutional conflicts:

Constitutional structure of popular sovereignty and democratic governance—The entire architecture of the American constitutional system rests on the premise that government derives its just powers from the consent of the governed, that citizens have the right to vote, to dissent, to petition, to protest, and to change their government through democratic processes. A principle of obligatory obedience to authority derived from divine mandate rather than popular consent is incompatible with this structure at the most fundamental level.

First Amendment—The rights of free speech, free press, and petition for redress of grievances are constitutional protections for political dissent—the right to criticize, oppose, and seek to remove those in authority. A divinely grounded obligation of political obedience directly contradicts these protections.

10.

تَحْرِيمُ سَبِّ النَّبِيِّ

Taḥrīm sabb al-nabī: **"Insulting the Prophet is forbidden—and punishable by death."**

This principle—elaborated definitively by Ibn Taymiyya in *Al-Ṣārim al-Maslūl ʿalā Shātim al-Rasūl* and grounded in Muhammad's own practice of ordering the killing of those who satirized or criticized him—is the foundation of classical Islamic blasphemy law. The prohibition covers any speech, writing, image, or gesture that could be construed as disrespectful toward Muhammad, the Quran, or Islam. The prescribed penalty in the dominant classical opinion is death—without the possibility of reprieve through repentance, because the offense, once committed, cannot be undone. The ruling applies to Muslims and non-Muslims alike and has been codified as statutory law in Pakistan (Section 295-C), Saudi Arabia, Iran, and elsewhere. It is the legal basis for the killing of Samuel Paty, the sentencing of Asia Bibi, and the Ayatollah's fatwa against Salman Rushdie.

Constitutional conflict:

First Amendment, Freedom of Speech—The First Amendment protects speech that is offensive, provocative, and deeply disturbing to its targets—including speech that criticizes, mocks, or rejects any religion or its founders. The Supreme Court has been unambiguous: there is no "hate speech" exception to the First Amendment, no category of protected religious figures whose honor the government may shield from criticism. A death penalty for speech that offends religious sensibility is the most complete possible contradiction of the First Amendment's foundational principle—that the government cannot silence ideas, however offensive, by the threat of punishment.

II.

دِيَةُ غَيْرِ الْمُسْلِمِ نِصْفُ دِيَةِ الْمُسْلِمِ

Diyat ghayr al-Muslim niṣf diyat al-Muslim: **"The blood money for a non-Muslim is half that of a Muslim."**

The *diya*—blood money, the financial compensation prescribed for killing or injuring another person—is explicitly set in classical sharia at different values depending on the religion of the victim. The full diya for a Muslim male is established by hadith at one hundred camels or its monetary equivalent. Under the Maliki, Hanbali, and Shafi'i schools, the diya for a Christian or Jewish victim is half this amount. The legal meaning is precise and inescapable: the life of a non-Muslim is worth, in the explicit calculus of Islamic jurisprudence, fifty percent of the life of a Muslim. This valuation is not an informal social prejudice or a cultural tendency. It is written law—the formal, jurisprudentially established monetary expression of the belief that non-Muslim lives carry lesser legal value.

Constitutional conflict:

Fourteenth Amendment, Equal Protection Clause—The Constitution's guarantee of equal protection rests on the premise that every person's life, safety, and bodily integrity are equally protected by the law regardless of religion. A legal system that assigns different monetary valuations to human lives based on the victim's faith violates equal protection as completely as it is possible to violate it. There is no half-price version of equal protection in the American constitutional tradition.

12.

لَا يُقْتَلُ مُسْلِمٌ بِكَافِرٍ

Lā yuqtalu Muslimun bi-kāfir: **"A Muslim is not to be executed for killing a non-Muslim."**

This ruling—recorded in *Sahih al-Bukhari* and accepted by the Hanafi, Maliki, and Hanbali schools—holds that a Muslim who kills a non-Muslim (*kafir*) does not face the *qisas* (retaliatory execution) that would apply if the victim were a Muslim. The Shafi'i school extends this protection further. The practical effect is that the killing of a non-Muslim by a Muslim carries a lesser legal consequence than the killing of a Muslim—both in terms of criminal liability and in the diya compensation owed to the victim's family. Combined with the diya differential described above, this ruling creates a comprehensive legal structure in which non-Muslim lives are protected less vigorously, compensated less generously, and avenged less severely than Muslim lives.

Constitutional conflict:

Fourteenth Amendment, Equal Protection Clause—The equal protection guarantee requires that the law protect every person's life with equal force regardless of their religion. A rule that exempts killers of non-Muslims from the capital penalty that would apply if their victim were Muslim assigns different legal value to different lives based on religion—a categorical violation of equal protection and a structural feature of exactly the kind of two-tiered legal citizenship that the Fourteenth Amendment was designed to abolish.

13.

تَحْرِيمُ الرِّدَّةِ وَالزَّنْدَقَةِ

Taḥrīm al-ridda wa-l-zandaqa: **"Apostasy and religious heresy are forbidden —and punishable by death."**

Beyond the specific ruling on changing one's religion addressed above, classical sharia's prohibition on *ridda* (apostasy) and zandaqa (heresy—the holding of beliefs that contradict Islamic orthodoxy while nominally remaining Muslim) creates a comprehensive system of enforced theological conformity. A Muslim who publicly questions the existence of God, denies the prophethood of Muhammad, rejects the authority of the Quran, or holds any of a range of beliefs deemed heretical by the classical scholars may be charged with zandaqa—a category that carries the death penalty and, in the dominant opinion, does not allow for the possibility of repentance, because the heretic's outward profession of Islam makes his inner rejection of it more dangerous to the community than open apostasy.

Constitutional conflict:

First Amendment, Free Exercise and Free Speech Clauses—The Constitution protects not only the right to practice a religion but the right to hold any beliefs—including heterodox, doubting, or rejecting beliefs—without government penalty. The freedom of conscience that the First Amendment protects is absolute: the government cannot prescribe what any person must believe, and it cannot punish the holding of unorthodox beliefs. A death penalty for theological heterodoxy is the complete negation of freedom of conscience.

14.

تَحْرِيمُ اللِّوَاطِ وَعُقُوبَتُهُ الْإِعْدَامُ

Taḥrīm al-liwāṭ wa-ʿuqūbatuhu al-iʿdām: **"Homosexuality is forbidden—and punishable by death."**

Muhammad's command—recorded in the hadith collections of Abu Dawud, al-Tirmidhi, and Ibn Majah—is explicit: "If you find anyone doing as Lot's people did, kill the one who does it and the one to whom it is done." Every major classical school of Sunni jurisprudence prescribes death for male homosexual intercourse, with variation only in the method—stoning, the sword, or throwing from a height, the last of these derived from a minority jurisprudential opinion that ISIS applied with systematic literalism in the territories it controlled. The ruling is applied as law in Saudi Arabia, Iran, Afghanistan, and other sharia-governed states, where gay men have been executed in the twenty-first century.

Constitutional conflicts:

Eighth Amendment — The Constitution prohibits cruel and unusual punishment. The death penalty for private consensual conduct between adults—whatever one's view of that conduct—constitutes cruel and unusual punishment by every standard the Supreme Court has articulated. No penological justification that American constitutional law recognizes can sustain a sentence of death for a non-violent act committed in private between consenting adults. The Eighth Amendment draws a categorical line between punishment and cruelty; classical sharia's prescribed execution for homosexual acts falls entirely on the wrong side of that line.

Fourteenth Amendment, Due Process and Equal Protection — The Constitution guarantees that every person stands equal before the law and that the state's coercive power over private life is not unlimited. In *Lawrence v. Texas* (2003), the Supreme Court held that criminal prohibition of consensual same-sex conduct between adults violates the constitutional right to liberty under the Due Process Clause. In *Obergefell v. Hodges* (2015), the Court recognized a constitutional right to same-sex marriage under both the Due

Process and Equal Protection Clauses. Whatever one's view of these decisions—and Americans continue to debate them—they reflect a foundational constitutional principle this book does not contest: that the state may not prescribe criminal punishment for private consensual conduct between adults, and that every person stands equal before the law regardless of the choices they make in private life. Classical sharia's prescription of death for homosexual acts is the complete negation of that principle—not a different approach to the same question, but the removal of every protection the Constitution in this area exists to provide.

15.

الْحَاكِمِيَّةُ لِلَّهِ وَحْدَهُ

Al-ḥākimiyya li-llāhi waḥdahu: **"Sovereignty belongs to Allah alone."**

This assertion is the foundational constitutional principle of classical Islamic political theology—the principle from which all the others flow. Derived from Quranic verses declaring that "judgment [or Legislation] belongs only to Allah" (Surah 12:40) and developed into a comprehensive political doctrine by scholars including Mawdudi and Qutb, *hakimiyya* holds that the ultimate authority to govern, legislate, and judge belongs exclusively to God. Human beings do not possess sovereignty. Legislatures do not possess sovereignty. Constitutions do not possess sovereignty—unless they derive their authority from divine revelation. Democracy, in this framework, is a form of *shirk*—the association of partners with God—because it attributes legislative sovereignty to human institutions. The Constitution of the United States, as a human document deriving its authority from popular consent rather than divine command, is, in classical Islamic political theology, an illegitimate usurpation of God's exclusive prerogative.

Constitutional conflict:

The entire constitutional order—The Constitution's Preamble locates sovereignty in "We the People." Its structure distributes governmental power among human institutions accountable to human citizens through democratic processes. Its amendment procedure allows the people themselves to change their governing framework through collective deliberation and consent. Every word of the Constitution rests on the premise that legitimate authority derives from the consent of the governed—the premise that *hakimiyya* directly and comprehensively denies. This difference is not a conflict between one provision of sharia and one provision of the Constitution. It is a conflict between two irreconcilable theories of political legitimacy—one human, one divine—that cannot both be true in the same society under the same law.

These fifteen principles are not a complete inventory of classical sharia's conflicts with the United States Constitution. They are its most direct and irreconcilable ones—the points where the two systems do not merely differ in approach or emphasis but hold opposite positions on the most fundamental questions of law, human dignity, and political authority. Each principle listed here is derived from primary Islamic sources—the Quran, the authenticated hadith, and the classical jurisprudential tradition—that are available to any reader through the digital resources listed in this book's bibliography. The author invites every reader to consult those sources directly and to judge for themselves whether the conflicts described here are real.

Arabic Principle	Plain Meaning	Primary Constitutional Conflict(s)
Lā wilāya li-ghayr al-Muslim ʿalā al-Muslim	No non-Muslim authority over Muslims	Article VI; 14th Amendment
Man baddala dīnahu fa-qtulūhu	Kill the apostate	1st Amendment; 8th Amendment
Dīn al-dawla al-Islām	Islam is the religion of the state	1st Amendment (Establishment Clause)
Al-jizya ʿalā ahl al-dhimma	Jizya tax on non-Muslims	14th Amendment (Equal Protection)
Shahādat al-marʾa niṣf shahādat al-rajul	Women's testimony worth half a man's	14th Amendment (Sex Equality)
Li-l-dhakari mithlu ḥaẓẓ al-unthayayn	Men inherit twice what women inherit	14th Amendment
Ḥadd al-sariqa qaṭʿ al-yad	Amputation of hand for theft	8th Amendment
Ḥadd al-zinā al-rajm li-l-muḥṣan	Stoning for adultery	8th Amendment; 14th Amendment
Wujūb ṭāʿat walī al-amr	Obligatory obedience to the ruler	Popular sovereignty; 1st Amendment
Taḥrīm sabb al-nabī	Death for insulting the Prophet	1st Amendment (Free Speech)
Diyat ghayr al-Muslim niṣf diyat al-Muslim	Non-Muslim blood money half of Muslim	14th Amendment (Equal Protection)
Lā yuqtalu Muslimun bi-kāfir	Muslim not executed for killing non-Muslim	14th Amendment (Equal Protection)
Taḥrīm al-ridda wa-l-zandaqa	Death for apostasy and for heresy	1st Amendment (Freedom of Conscience)
Taḥrīm al-liwāṭ wa-ʿuqūbatuhu al-iʿdām	Death for homosexual acts	14th Amendment; 8th Amendment
Al-ḥākimiyya li-llāhi waḥdahu	Sovereignty belongs to Allah alone	Entire constitutional order

GLOSSARY

The following terms appear throughout this book. Each is defined here in its classical Islamic legal sense—the sense in which it is used in the primary sources and in the jurisprudential tradition that Islamist movements cite as their authority.

Apostasy *(Arabic: Ridda or Irtidad)*: The act of leaving Islam—abandoning the Islamic faith after having embraced it, whether by converting to another religion, by declaring oneself an atheist, or by any conduct that Islamic jurisprudence interprets as equivalent to rejection of the faith. Under classical sharia, apostasy is a capital offense for which the prescribed penalty in all four major Sunni schools of jurisprudence is death, following a period in which the apostate is given the opportunity to recant. The foundational legal basis is Muhammad's hadith recorded in *Sahih al-Bukhari*: "Whoever changes his Islamic religion, kill him."

Bid'a: Innovation in religious matters—the introduction of claims, practices, or beliefs not found in the Quran, the hadith, or the established traditions of the early Muslim community. Classical Islamic jurisprudence regards *bid'a* as forbidden, and Salafi and Wahhabi movements treat the prohibition on *bid'a* as the basis for their rejection of any theological development that departs from the literal meaning of the primary sources and the earliest practices of Muhammad and his companions. This principle is relevant to this book's argument because it explains why the classical rulings on apostasy, blasphemy, and the treatment of non-Muslims cannot simply be reformed away within the framework of classical sharia—any departure from the established rulings is itself *bid'a*.

Blasphemy: In classical Islamic jurisprudence, the act of insulting, mocking, or criticizing Muhammad, the Quran, or Islam. The prescribed penalty in the dominant classical opinion—as argued by Ibn Taymiyya in his infamous book *al-Sarim al-Maslul*—is death, with no possibility of reprieve through repentance. The ruling applies to Muslims and non-Muslims alike and has been applied historically to poets, writers, scholars, and ordinary individuals who expressed criticism of Islamic doctrine or Islam's prophet. Contemporary blasphemy laws in Pakistan, Saudi Arabia, Iran, and other Muslim-majority countries derive directly from this classical jurisprudential tradition.

Caliphate *(Arabic: Khilafa)*: The classical Islamic political institution representing the unified governance of the global Muslim community—the umma—under a single leader, the Caliph (*Khalifa*), who derives his authority from his role as guardian of Islamic law and successor to the religious and political authority of Muhammad. The last widely recognized caliphate was the Ottoman caliphate, abolished by Mustafa Kemal Atatürk in 1924. The restoration of the caliphate is a stated goal of Islamist movements including the Muslim Brotherhood and was the specific claim of ISIS when it declared its "Islamic State" in 2014.

Dar al-Harb *(House of War)*: In classical Islamic political theology, the territories not governed by sharia—literally "the house of war," meaning territories that are in a state of potential or actual conflict with the Islamic world. The United States, in this framework, is *dar al-harb*. The classical obligation of the Muslim community is to transform *dar al-harb* into *dar al-Islam* through dawah, political action, or, historically, military conquest.

Dar al-Islam *(House of Islam)*: In classical Islamic political theology, the territories governed by sharia. The classical obligation of Muslim governance is to expand *dar al-Islam* until Islamic law governs all of humanity.

Dawah: Literally "invitation" or "call"—the Islamic practice of calling people to Islam. In classical jurisprudence, dawah is an obligation on the Muslim community and the first step in the process of bringing non-Muslim territo ries under Islamic governance. In contemporary Islamist strategy in the West, dawah encompasses not only personal religious invitation but the broader project of establishing Islamic institutional infrastructure—mosques, schools, advocacy organizations, political presence—designed to expand Islam's social and political influence.

Dhimmi: The legal status assigned under classical sharia to Christians and Jews—"People of the Book"—living under Islamic governance. The term derives from the Arabic for "obligation" or "protection"—the Islamic state undertakes an obligation to protect dhimmis from killing, in exchange for their payment of the jizya and their acceptance of a comprehensive set of legal, social, and religious disabilities. These disabilities include reduced *diya* (blood money), inadmissible or discounted court testimony, prohibition on building new houses of worship, prohibition on holding authority over Muslims, and various restrictions on public religious expression. The Quranic basis for the dhimmi system is Surah 9:29, which commands that the jizya be collected until the non-Muslim "feels himself subdued."

Diya *(Blood Money)*: The financial compensation prescribed by Islamic law for killing or injuring another person. The full diya for a Muslim male is set by hadith at one hundred camels or its monetary equivalent. According to various sharia precepts, the diya for a dhimmi—a Christian or Jewish victim—is half that of a Muslim victim, reflecting the lower legal valuation of non-Muslim life in classical sharia.

Fatwa: A formal legal ruling issued by a qualified Islamic scholar (*mufti*) in response to a question about Islamic law. A fatwa is not legislation in the Western sense—it is an authoritative scholarly opinion that carries binding weight for those who accept the issuing scholar's authority. The Ayatollah Khomeini's 1989 fatwa calling for the death of Salman Rushdie is perhaps the most internationally known example of a fatwa's real-world consequences.

Fiqh: Islamic jurisprudence—the human science of understanding the sharia and deriving legal rulings from the primary sources of sharia (Quran and Hadith) and applying them to specific circumstances related to life and worship. The classical schools of fiqh—Hanafi, Maliki, Shafiʿi, and Hanbali in the Sunni tradition; Jaʾfari in the Shiʿi tradition—represent different methodological traditions for this interpretive work. The rulings of the classical fiqh schools are what this book refers to when it speaks of "classical sharia."

Hakimiyya *(Divine Sovereignty)*: The doctrine that sovereignty—the ultimate authority to govern and legislate—belongs exclusively to Allah. *Hakimiyya* is the foundational principle of Islamist political theology, derived from Quranic verses declaring that "judgment belongs only to Allah" (Surah 12:40) and used by classical, modern, and contemporary Muslim scholars to argue that democracy—which locates sovereignty in the people—is incompatible with Islamic governance.

Hadith: The recorded sayings, actions, and tacit approvals of Islam's prophet, Muhammad, compiled by Islamic scholars in the generations after his death and authenticated through rigorous chains of transmission (*isnad*). The hadith, alongside the Quran, constitute the primary sources of Islamic law. The most authoritative Sunni hadith collections—*Sahih al-Bukhari* and *Sahih Muslim*—are designated *sahih* (sound, reliable, and authentic) and their contents carry binding legal authority in classical jurisprudence.

Hudud *(Singular: Hadd)*: The category of punishments prescribed directly by the Quran and hadith for specific offenses, with fixed penalties that human judges have no authority to reduce or set aside. The hudud offenses and their prescribed penalties include: theft (amputation of the right hand); fornication (one hundred lashes); adultery by a married person (stoning to death); false accusation of adultery (eighty lashes); drinking alcohol (eighty lashes in the majority opinion); highway robbery (amputation, crucifixion, or death); and apostasy (death). The fixed, divine origin of these penalties means they are, in classical jurisprudence, permanently beyond human legislative revision.

Ijma *(Islamic Scholarly Consensus)*: One of the four classical sources of Islamic law, especially among the Sunnis, alongside the Quran, the Hadith, and *qiyas* (analogical reasoning). *Ijma* refers to the consensus of Islamic scholars on a given legal question. When the classical jurists reached consensus on a ruling—such as the death penalty for apostasy—that consensus carries particularly strong legal authority and is especially resistant to reform, because overturning it requires not merely reinterpreting a text but arguing against the accumulated judgment of the entire tradition.

ISIS: The Islamic State of Iraq and Syria; a jihadist organization that controlled significant territory in Iraq and Syria from 2014 to 2019 and declared itself a restored caliphate. ISIS applied classical sharia punishments with systematic literalism, including public amputations, stonings, and executions for apostasy and homosexuality.

Islamism: The Islamic ideological disposition that seeks to establish sharia as the governing law of society and the state. Distinct from simply being a personal faith, Islamism treats Islamic law as a comprehensive political program and pursues its implementation through various means—political participation, legal advocacy, cultural transformation, and in some expressions, violence. Major Islamist organizations include the Muslim Brotherhood (founded in Egypt in 1928), Taliban, Hamas, Hezbollah, al-Qaeda, and ISIS, as well as numerous ostensibly non-violent organizations operating in Western democracies.

Islamophobia: A term used to describe prejudice or hostility toward Muslims as people. While genuine anti-Muslim bigotry exists and deserves condemnation, the term is frequently deployed by Islamist advocacy organizations to shield Islamic political doctrine from legitimate scrutiny. This book distinguishes between hostility toward Muslim people, which it rejects, and honest examination of Islamic law, which it practices.

Jahiliyya: Literally "ignorance"—in classical Islamic usage, the condition of pre-Islamic Arabia before the advent of Muhammad and the revelation of the Quran. Sayyid Qutb used the term to describe any society—including Muslim-majority societies—that does not govern itself by sharia, arguing that the entire modern world is in a state of *jahiliyya* equivalent to pre-Islamic barbarism.

Jihad: Literally "struggle" or "striving." In classical Islamic jurisprudence, jihad has always been linked to fighting on the battlefield in Allah's cause and in his path. Later Muslims created an additional layer, suggesting twofold meanings—an internal dimension (the personal struggle against moral failure) and an external dimension (the collective effort to expand the domain of Islamic governance through tactics or through warring). The external jihad—military struggle to extend *dar al-Islam*, replacing and suppressing *dar al-Harb*—is a collective obligation (*fard kifaya*) in classical sharia, fulfilled when a sufficient portion of the Muslim community undertakes it. Contemporary Islamist movements apply the concept of jihad to the full range of strategies for advancing Islamic governance, including non-violent political and cultural action.

Jizya: The poll tax levied on dhimmis—Christians and Jews—living under Islamic governance, prescribed in Surah 9:29. The jizya is not a neutral tax but a performative instrument of subordination—classical Muslim commentators specify that it must be paid in a manner that humiliates the payer, marking his acceptance of Islamic supremacy and emphasizing his own second-class status. The jizya symbolizes the dhimmi's submission to Islamic governance as a condition of his continued toleration.

Kafir *(Plural: Kuffar or Kafirun)*: This term refers to the unbeliever—i.e., any non-Muslim—whereas the term *kufr* means disbelief, the rejection of Islam. A kafir is a person who rejects the Islamic faith, in part or altogether. The term carries severe theological and legal implications in classical sharia, as the kafir lacks the full legal protections that Islamic law grants to Muslims. A kafir is a stigma in Muslim circles. Christians and Jews occupy a particular subcategory as *ahl al-kitab* (People of the Book), which grants them conditional toleration through the dhimmi system, although they are also described by Muslim jurists as polytheists or infidels, based on some verses from the Quran. Under sharia, polytheists and atheists receive no toleration.

Murtad: An apostate—a Muslim who has abandoned Islam. The *murtad* is subject, under classical sharia, to the death penalty following a period in which he is urged to repent. A subcategory defines a *murtad harbi*—an apostate who actively works against Islam—this is to be killed immediately without the waiting period. A *murtad milla*—an apostate who simply leaves the faith—is given the opportunity to return before the sentence is carried out.

Muslim Brotherhood (*al-Ikhwan al-Muslimun*): A transnational Islamist organization founded in Egypt in 1928 by Hassan al-Banna, originally in response to the abolition of the Ottoman caliphate and the perceived encroachment of Western secular influence on Muslim societies. The Brotherhood is widely regarded as the grandfather organization of modern Islamist political movements — the ideological source from which Hamas, and numerous other Islamist organizations across the Middle East, Europe, and North America trace their founding inspiration or organizational lineage. Its foundational goal, stated in its own founding documents and elaborated by its most influential theorist Sayyid Qutb, is the establishment of Islamic governance under sharia as the comprehensive legal and political order of society. In the United States, the Brotherhood's strategic objectives were laid out in a 1991 internal document describing its mission as "a kind of grand Jihad in eliminating and destroying the Western civilization from within and 'sabotaging' its miserable house by their hands and the hands of the believers so that it is eliminated and God's religion is made victorious over all other religions." Several Western governments have designated the Brotherhood or its affiliates as terrorist organizations; the United States has not done so as of this writing, though the question has been debated in Congress. The Brotherhood's American network has been said to include organizations such as ISNA and CAIR. In the 2007–2008 Holy Land Foundation trial, the government named both as unindicted co-conspirators and introduced evidence of their association with HLF and Hamas; the presiding judge found 'ample evidence' of that association. None of these organizations was charged or convicted, however, and a federal court subsequently held that the government's public naming of them violated their due-process rights. Both organizations dispute any such ties.

Nikah: An Islamic marriage contract, although the term also refers to sexual intercourse. Under classical sharia, the *nikah* includes specific provisions regarding the *mahr* (bride gift), the husband's control and rights over the wife's conduct, and the conditions under which divorce may be obtained. The asymmetry of the *nikah*—in which the husband has the right of unilateral divorce (*talaq*) while the wife must generally seek the husband's consent or a court ruling—is one of the most significant points of conflict between classical sharia family law and the equal protection principles of American constitutional law.

OIC: The Organization of Islamic Cooperation; an intergovernmental body of 57 member states representing the collective voice of the Muslim world in international affairs. The OIC has consistently advocated for international restrictions on criticism of Islam.

Qiyas *(Analogical Reasoning)*: One of the four classical sources of Islamic law, used to extend the rulings of the Quran and hadith to situations not explicitly addressed by the primary texts. Through *qiyas*, Islamic jurists have derived rulings on topics ranging from the permissibility of new foods and technologies to the legal treatment of novel social situations—always by analogy to established precedents in the primary sources.

Salafism: A movement within Sunni Islam that advocates returning to the practice of the *salaf*—the first three generations of Muslims—as the authoritative model for Islamic life and law. A Salafi is a Muslim who strives to live Islam as described and exemplified in the earliest three generations of Islam. Salafism treats the primary sources and the practice of the early community—especially the traditions attributed to Muhammad and his immediate companions—as normative and binding, rejecting later theological and legal developments as potentially corrupting innovations. Salafism is the theological foundation of Saudi Wahhabism and of many contemporary Islamist movements. It is directly relevant to this book because Salafi jurisprudence most consistently reflects the classical rulings—on apostasy, blasphemy, hudud, and the treatment of non-Muslims—that this book has examined.

Sahih: The Arabic term meaning "sound" or "reliable," used in Islamic hadith scholarship to designate reports that have passed the classical criteria for authenticity established by Muslim scholars in the eighth and ninth centuries. A hadith classified as *sahih* is considered the highest grade of reliability within the Islamic scholarly tradition: its chain of transmission (*isnad*) has been evaluated and accepted as unbroken, and each transmitter in the chain has been assessed as trustworthy by the classical scholars who developed the science of hadith criticism (*ʿilm al-rijal*). The two most authoritative Sunni hadith collections—*Sahih al-Bukhari* and *Sahih Muslim*—take their names from this designation, reflecting their compilers' claim that every hadith they contain meets the *sahih* standard. Throughout this book, *sahih* hadiths are cited as primary sources for Islamic legal rulings because they are the reports that classical jurists have treated as binding—the reports on which the rulings examined here are actually based. The term reflects a classification internal to the Islamic scholarly tradition. It does not imply independent historical verification by the standards of modern Western historiography, and Western scholars of early Islam have raised substantive questions about the hadith tradition as a whole. The book's argument does not depend on resolving those debates: it depends on the fact that these reports are accepted as authoritative by the tradition that produced the legal rulings this book documents, and that they are cited as such by Islamist movements operating in the United States today.

Sharia: Literally "the straight path"—Islamic divine law, derived from the Quran and the Sunna (Muhammad's example as documented in the hadith), explained and elaborated through the jurisprudential tradition of fiqh, and governing all aspects of Muslim religious, personal, social, political, and legal life. Sharia is not a single book but a comprehensive legal tradition developed over fourteen centuries of scholarship. In its classical and authoritative form—the form that Islamist movements cite as their basis—sharia establishes the legal hierarchies, political doctrines, and criminal penalties examined throughout this book. As Allah's law, Muslims believe that sharia applies on Muslims and non-Muslims alike.

Shirk: The gravest sin in Islamic theology—associating partners with Allah, attributing divine qualities or divine authority to anything other than Allah. In classical *hakimiyya* doctrine, democracy is a form of *shirk* because it attributes legislative sovereignty—which belongs exclusively to Allah—to human beings and their institutions.

Sunna: The practice and example of Muhammad—his words, actions, and tacit approvals—as documented in the hadith collections. The Sunna, alongside the Quran, is the foundational source of Islamic law. Whatever Muhammad said or did is considered sacred and mandatory to imitate—this is a principle that governs classical Islamic jurisprudence at every level.

Takfir: The act of declaring a Muslim to be an apostate or unbeliever (kafir). In classical jurisprudence, *takfir* carries severe consequences, as a Muslim declared kafir loses the legal protections that Islamic law affords believers. Islamist movements have historically used *takfir* as a weaponizing tool for justifying violence against Muslims who are deemed insufficiently observant or who support secular governance.

Talaq: The Islamic divorce—specifically, the husband's right of unilateral divorce by declaration. Under classical sharia, a husband may divorce his wife by pronouncing the word *talaq* ("I divorce you") three times, with varying procedural requirements across the schools. A wife generally cannot obtain a divorce without either her husband's consent or a ruling from a sharia court—an asymmetry that places women at a significant disadvantage in marriage dissolution and that has been extensively documented in the operations of sharia councils in Britain and elsewhere.

Tafsir: Quranic commentary—the scholarly discipline of interpreting the meaning of Quranic verses. The classical tafsir works, particularly those of al-Tabari, al-Qurtubi, and Ibn Kathir represent the authoritative tradition of Quranic interpretation that Islamic legal scholars draw upon in deriving legal rulings from the text. The tafsir of the legally significant verses cited throughout this book—on divine sovereignty, the jizya, the treatment of women, and the hudud penalties—reflects the consensus of classical Islamic scholarship on their meaning.

Umma: The global community of Muslims—all believers, regardless of national origin, ethnicity, or language, united by their faith in Allah and their adherence to Muhammad's example. In Islamist political theology, loyalty to the umma supersedes loyalty to any nation-state or earthly constitution. The concept of the umma is the theological basis for the transnational character of Islamist movements and for their view of Muslim communities in Western democracies as outposts of the global Islamic community rather than as citizens of their host nations.

Wahhabism: A strict reform movement within Sunni Islam founded by Muhammad ibn Abd al-Wahhab in eighteenth-century Arabia and adopted as the official theology of the Saudi state. Wahhabism advocates a literal reading of the primary sources, the elimination of practices deemed innovations, and the full implementation of classical sharia including its criminal punishments. The Saudi state's export of Wahhabi doctrine—through the funding of mosques and Islamist organizations worldwide—has been one of the most significant factors in the global spread of Islamist movements over the past five decades.

Wilaya *(Guardianship/Authority)*: The concept of legal guardianship or authority in Islamic law. The principle *La wilaya li-ghayr al-Muslim ala al-Muslim*—"no authority for a non-Muslim over a Muslim"—is a foundational rule of classical sharia that prohibits non-Muslims from holding positions of authority over Muslims in any domain of governance, judiciary, or public administration. This principle is directly incompatible with the equal protection and equal citizenship guarantees of the United States Constitution.

Zakat: The obligatory annual charitable contribution prescribed by Islamic law—one of the Five Pillars of Islam. Zakat is paid by Muslims on their accumulated wealth above a minimum threshold and distributed to specified categories of recipients. Unlike the jizya—which is a marker of non-Muslim subordination—zakat is an internal Islamic religious obligation with no parallel legal discrimination embedded in it. It is listed here to illustrate the contrast between sharia's genuinely personal religious obligations and its political-legal ones.

This glossary reflects the classical, authoritative meanings of these terms as used in the primary sources and jurisprudential tradition examined throughout this book. Granted, some individual Muslims may understand and use some of these terms differently in personal or informal contexts. The meanings given here are those that govern classical Islamic jurisprudence and that Islamist movements invoke as the basis for their political and legal advocacy.

REFERENCES

This book is generally without a scholarly apparatus, since most facts can be easily discovered. However, knowing that some readers prefer references, citations substantiating major claims are listed below.

INTRODUCTION

p. xxvi Google Trends, "Sharia Law," search query for the United States, January 2022–June 2026, https://trends.google.com/explore?q=sharia%20law&date=2022-01-01%202026-06-26&geo=US, accessed June 2026.

p. xxvi "A Closer Look at Sharia in the United States," Islamic Networks Group, https://ing.org/resources/a-closer-look-at-sharia-in-the-united-states/, accessed June 2026.

pp. xxvi–xxvii "Preserving a Sharia-Free America Act," H.R. 5722, 119th Congress, https://www.congress.gov/bill/119th-congress/house-bill/5722, accessed June 2026. See also Keith Self and Chip Roy, "Congressmen Keith Self and Chip Roy Launch Sharia-Free America Caucus," press release, https://keithself.house.gov/media/press-releases/congressmen-keith-self-and-chip-roy-launch-sharia-free-america-caucus, accessed June 2026.

p. xxvii J.L. Partners for the Heritage Foundation, "US Muslims Polling," September 2024, https://jlpartners.com/us-muslims-polling-for-the-heritage-foundation, accessed June 2026. Nationally representative sample of 1,000 Americans and 1,000 US Muslims, September 6–13, 2024.

CHAPTER 1

p. 4 MEMRI (Middle East Media Research Institute), "Islamic Scholars at AIM Conference: Islam Will Rule the World—America Will Be a Muslim Country," https://www.memri.org/tv/islamic-scholars-aim-conference-islam-rule-world-america-muslim-country, accessed June 2026. For additional examples, see MEMRI TV, Sermons by Imams in the West, https://www.memri.org/tv/subjects/sermons-by-imams-in-the-west, accessed June 2026.

p. 6 Mohamed Akram, "An Explanatory Memorandum on the General Strategic Goal for the Group in North America," May 22, 1991, Government Exhibit 003-0085, United States v. Holy Land Foundation for Relief and Development, No. 3:04-CR-240-G (N.D. Tex. 2007), https://www.documentcloud.org/documents/228562-elbarasse-search-3/, accessed June 2026. See also the full text at the Investigative Project on Terrorism, https://www.investigativeproject.org/document/20-an-explanatory-memorandum-on-the-general, accessed June 2026.

p. 7 Adam Sabes, "Qatar, Saudi Arabia Sent Billions to US Universities, Report Finds," *Campus Reform*, https://www.campusreform.org/article/qatar-saudi-arabia-sent-billions-us-universities-report-finds/29709, accessed June 2026.

CHAPTER 2

p. 12 "Whoever changes his Islamic religion, kill him": *Sahih al-Bukhari*, Vol. 9, Book 84, Hadith 57, https://sunnah.com/bukhari:6922, accessed June 2026.

p. 12 Ukl tribe: *Sahih al-Bukhari*, Vol. 8, Book 82, Hadith 797, https://sunnah.com/bukhari:6805, accessed June 2026.

p. 13 On the Ridda Wars, see A.S. Ibrahim, *The Stated Motivations for the Early Islamic Conquests*, ch. 4; and Hugh Kennedy, *The Prophet and the Age of the Caliphates*, 2nd ed. (London: Longman, 2004).

p. 13–14 Al-Nawawi, *Minhaj al-Talibin*, trans. E.C. Howard (London: W. Thacker, 1914). The passage "when a Muslim apostatizes from Islam, the imam asks him to repent" appears in Book XI (Apostasy). See also the online translation at https://sunnah.com, accessed June 2026.

p. 14 Ibn Qudama, *Al-Mughni* (Riyadh: Dar 'Alam al-Kutub, 1997), vol. 9.

See also "Punishment for Apostasy in Islam," *Islam Q&A*, https://islamqa.info/en/answers/14231/punishment-for-apostasy-in-islam, accessed June 2026.

pp. 14–15 Pew Research Center, "Laws Penalizing Blasphemy, Apostasy and Defamation of Religion Are Widespread," August 9, 2011, https://www.pewresearch.org/religion/2011/08/09/rising-restrictions-on-religion6/, accessed June 2026.

p. 15 On Meriam Ibrahim, see US Commission on International Religious Freedom, "USCIRF Strongly Condemns Apostasy Prosecution of Sudanese Woman," https://www.uscirf.gov/news-room/releases-statements/uscirf-strongly-condemns-apostasy-prosecution-sudanese-woman, accessed June 2026. See also Sarah Sirgany and Laura Smith-Spark, "Meriam Ibrahim, Facing Execution in Sudan, Arrives in New Hampshire," *CNN*, July 31, 2014, https://www.cnn.com/2014/07/31/us/new-hampshire-sudanese-woman, accessed June 2026.

p. 15 On Raif Badawi, see Amnesty International USA, "Flogged for Blogging," https://www.amnestyusa.org/cases/flogged-for-blogging/, accessed June 2026. See also *CNN*, "Saudi Blogger Sentenced to 1,000 Lashes, 10 Years in Prison," May 7, 2014, https://www.cnn.com/2014/05/07/world/meast/saudi-activist-sentenced, accessed June 2026.

CHAPTER 3

p. 22 Kaʿb ibn al-Ashraf: *Sahih al-Bukhari*, Vol. 4, Book 52, Hadith 270–271, https://sunnah.com/bukhari:3031 and https://sunnah.com/bukhari:3032, accessed June 2026.

p. 25 Pakistan Penal Code Section 295-C, as amended 1986, https://www.pakistani.org/pakistan/legislation/1860/actXLVof1860.html, accessed June 2026.

pp. 25–26 On Asia Bibi, see "Asia Bibi: The Christian Woman at the Centre of Pakistan's Blasphemy Row," *BBC News*, October 31, 2018, https://www.bbc.com/news/world-asia-46040515, accessed June 2026. For the Supreme Court judgment, see *Mst. Aasia Bibi v. The State*, Criminal Appeal No. 39-L/2015, Supreme Court of Pakistan, https://web.archive.org/web/20181031151312/http://www.supremecourt.gov.pk/web/user_files/File/Crl.A._39_L_2015.pdf, accessed June 2026.

p. 26 Ayatollah Khomeini fatwa against Salman Rushdie, February 14,

1989: English translation and Persian original at Iran Data Portal, Syracuse University, https://irandataportal.syr.edu/fatwa-against-salman-rushdie/, accessed June 2026.

p. 26 On Rushdie's translators and publishers: Japanese translator Hitoshi Igarashi—"*Satanic Verses* Translator Found Slain," *Washington Post*, July 13, 1991, https://www.washingtonpost.com/archive/politics/1991/07/13/satanic-verses-translator-found-slain/6ee67d24-9b02-4eaf-994e-107ff814f64f/, accessed June 2026. Italian translator Ettore Capriolo—ABC News, "The Fatwa Against Author Salman Rushdie Led to 30 Years of Terror," https://abcnews.go.com/International/fatwa-author-salman-rushdie-led-30-years-terror/story?id=88355931, accessed June 2026. Norwegian publisher William Nygaard—*The Guardian*, November 26, 2010, https://www.theguardian.com/books/2010/nov/26/norwegian-publisher-william-nygaard, accessed June 2026.

p. 27 On Samuel Paty, see "Samuel Paty: France Pays Tribute to Beheaded Teacher," *BBC News*, October 21, 2020, https://www.bbc.com/news/world-europe-54632353, accessed June 2026.

p. 27 On Kurt Westergaard, see "Somali Charged in Danish Cartoonist Attack," *CBS News*, January 4, 2010, https://www.cbsnews.com/news/somali-charged-in-danish-cartoonist-attack/, accessed June 2026.

p. 30 On vigilante killings under Pakistan's blasphemy laws, see Human Rights Watch, *World Report 2024: Pakistan*, https://www.hrw.org/world-report/2024/country-chapters/pakistan, accessed June 2026.

p. 30 On Al-Azhar and the classical death penalty for blasphemy, see Rudolph Peters and Gert J.J. De Vries, "Apostasy in Islam," *Die Welt des Islams* 17 (1976): 1–25. See also "Killing Apostates Condoned," *Washington Post*, July 22, 1993, https://www.washingtonpost.com/archive/politics/1993/07/22/killing-apostates-condoned/68d0d42a-958f-4f42-8ad2-666a1629e2a0/, accessed June 2026.

p. 30 Criminal Justice and Immigration Act 2008, sec. 79 (UK), https://www.legislation.gov.uk/ukpga/2008/4/section/79, accessed June 2026. The provision abolishing the common law offences of blasphemy and blasphemous libel came into force July 8, 2008.

CHAPTER 4

pp. 34–35 Muhammad on women's deficiency in intelligence and religion: *Sahih al-Bukhari*, Vol. 1, Book 6, Hadith 301, https://sunnah.com/bukhari:304, accessed June 2026.

p. 35 "A people who place a woman in charge of their affairs will never succeed": *Sahih al-Bukhari*, Vol. 9, Book 88, Hadith 219, https://sunnah.com/bukhari:7099, accessed June 2026.

p. 37 Ibn Kathir's commentary on Surah 9:29, including the description of jizya payment with humiliation, is available at Alim.org, https://www.alim.org/quran/tafsir/ibn-kathir/surah/9/0/, accessed June 2026.

p. 38 On diya amounts in classical sharia, see "Diyah," *Encyclopaedia Britannica*, https://www.britannica.com/topic/diyah, accessed June 2026. For a Muslim jurisprudential discussion, see "It Is Not Permissible to Waive the Diyah if the Slain Person Was in Debt," *Islam Q&A*, https://islamqa.info/en/answers/146907/it-is-not-permissible-to-waive-the-diyah-if-the-slain-person-was-in-debt, accessed June 2026.

p. 40 On the Pact of Umar, see "The Pact of Umar," in *Medieval Sourcebook*, Hanover Historical Texts Project, https://history.hanover.edu/courses/excerpts/211umar.html, accessed June 2026. See also A.S. Tritton, *The Caliphs and Their Non-Muslim Subjects* (London: Oxford University Press, 1930); and Milka Levy-Rubin, *Non-Muslims in the Early Islamic Empire* (Cambridge: Cambridge University Press, 2011).

CHAPTER 5

p. 48 On Saudi judicial amputations in the twenty-first century, see Human Rights Watch, "Saudi Arabia: Save Convict from Amputation," December 16, 2011, https://www.hrw.org/news/2011/12/16/saudi-arabia-save-convict-amputation, accessed June 2026.

pp. 50–51 Pakistan's Offence of Zina (Enforcement of Hudood) Ordinance, 1979, https://pakistani.org/pakistan/legislation/hudood.html, accessed June 2026.

p. 51 Muhammad personally ordering and supervising stonings: *Sahih al-Bukhari*, Vol. 8, Book 82, Hadith 816, https://sunnah.com/bukhari:6829, accessed June 2026; *Sahih Muslim*, Book 17, Hadith 4214, https://sunnah.com/muslim:1700a, accessed June 2026.

pp. 51–52 On stoning sentences and executions in Iran, Saudi Arabia, Afghanistan, Sudan, and Nigeria, see Amnesty International, "Death Penalty in 2025: Facts and Figures," May 2026, https://www.amnesty.org/en/

latest/news/2026/05/death-penalty-in-2025-facts-and-figures/, accessed June 2026.

p. 53 On Mahmoud Asgari and Ayaz Marhoni, see "Iran 'Executes Gay Teenagers,'" *BBC News*, July 22, 2005, http://news.bbc.co.uk/2/hi/middle_east/4725959.stm, accessed June 2026. See also Iran Human Rights Memorial, https://www.iranrights.org/memorial/story/35819/mahmud-asgari, accessed June 2026.

p. 53 On ISIS executing homosexual men by throwing them from rooftops, see NBC News, "ISIS Hurls Gay Men Off Buildings, Stones Them: Analysts," https://www.nbcnews.com/storyline/isis-uncovered/isis-hurls-gay-men-buildings-stones-them-analysts-n305171, accessed June 2026.

CHAPTER 6

pp. 59–60 Sayyid Qutb, *Milestones* (*Ma'alim fi al-Tariq*) (Indianapolis: American Trust Publications, 1990).

p. 60 On Khamenei's Farsi translation of *Milestones*, see "Iran's Leadership and the Muslim Brotherhood," American Sephardi Federation, June 2022, https://americansephardi.org/news/simjune22/, accessed June 2026. See also Gilles Kepel, *Muslim Extremism in Egypt: The Prophet and Pharaoh* (Berkeley: University of California Press, 1985).

p. 60 On Mawdudi and the modern systematization of hakimiyya, see Sohail Hashmi, "Locating Ḥākimiyya in Global History," *Journal of the Royal Asiatic Society* 32, no. 1 (2022), https://www.cambridge.org/core/journals/journal-of-the-royal-asiatic-society/article/abs/locating-hakimiyya-in-global-history-the-concept-of-sovereignty-in-premodern-islam-and-its-reception-after-mawdudi-and-qutb/925D58BDAE0F23128346B6730F8679ED, accessed June 2026. See also Abu al-Ala Mawdudi, *The Islamic Law and Constitution*, trans. Khurshid Ahmad (Lahore: Islamic Publications, 1955).

p. 66 On ISIS's 2014 caliphate declaration and the flow of foreign recruits, see The Soufan Group, *Foreign Fighters: An Updated Assessment of the Flow of Foreign Fighters into Syria and Iraq* (New York: The Soufan Group, 2015).

CHAPTER 7

p. 73 Rowan Williams, "Civil and Religious Law in England: A Religious Perspective," lecture at the Royal Courts of Justice, London, February 7, 2008. Full text at the Middle East Forum, https://www.meforum.org/islamist-watch/full-text-of-archbishops-lecture-civil, accessed June 2026.

pp. 74–75 Dame Louise Casey, *The Casey Review: A Review into Opportunity and Integration* (London: HMSO, December 2016). See also parliamentary debate: Hansard, House of Commons, December 6, 2016, https://hansard.parliament.uk/commons/2016-12-06/debates/FF91364D-4324-4420-943A-5ABCE8C9ADD1/CaseyReport, accessed June 2026.

p. 78 *Jabri v. Qaddura*, 108 S.W.3d 404 (Tex. App.—Fort Worth 2003), https://law.justia.com/cases/texas/second-court-of-appeals/2003/14601.html, accessed June 2026.

p. 78 *Hosain v. Malik*, 108 Md. App. 284, 671 A.2d 988 (Md. Ct. Spec. App. 1996), https://law.justia.com/cases/maryland/court-of-special-appeals/1996/228s95.html, accessed June 2026.

pp. 78–79 *S.D. v. M.J.R.*, 2 A.3d 412 (N.J. Super. Ct. App. Div. 2010), https://caselaw.findlaw.com/court/nj-superior-court-appellate-division/1532706.html, accessed June 2026.

BIBLIOGRAPHY OF PRIMARY SOURCES AND FURTHER READING

The sources listed in this bibliography are not suggestions for academic specialists. They are an invitation to every American who wants to verify, with their own eyes, that the arguments made in this book rest on exactly what they claim to rest on—the primary texts of Islam, read in their authoritative form, available to anyone with an internet connection. The age of "you have to trust the scholar" is over. The sources are accessible. The translations are available. The rulings are documented. What follows is a guide to finding them.

The bibliography is organized in three sections: (1) digital resources for primary source access, (2) classical primary texts referenced throughout this book, and (3) selected scholarly secondary works. The digital resources are listed first because they are the most immediately accessible to lay readers and because the argument of this book depends not on taking any scholar's word—including the author's—but on reading what the sources actually say.

PART ONE: DIGITAL RESOURCES FOR PRIMARY SOURCE ACCESS

Hadith Collections

Sunnah.com *https://sunnah.com/*

This is the single most important website for any reader who wants to access the authenticated traditions of Muhammad directly. Sunnah.com hosts the complete texts of the major hadith collections in both Arabic and English translation, fully searchable by keyword, topic, narrator, and authenticity grade. The collections available include *Sahih al-Bukhari*, *Sahih Muslim*, *Sunan Abu Dawud*, *Jami al-Tirmidhi*, *Sunan Ibn Majah*, *Sunan al-Nasa'i*, and several others—together comprising the foundational corpus of authenticated prophetic traditions that classical Islamic jurisprudence draws upon. Every hadith cited in this book—Muhammad's command to kill the apostate, his ordering of assassinations for those who insulted him, his rulings on women's testimony, his prescriptions for the treatment of non-Muslims—can be verified here in seconds. The site's search function allows readers to enter keywords in English and locate the relevant hadith with its full chain of transmission, its authenticity classification, and its cross-references across multiple collections. For anyone who wants to move beyond secondary sources and read Muhammad's recorded words directly, Sunnah.com is indispensable.

Sahih-Bukhari.com *https://www.sahih-bukhari.com/*

This site is dedicated specifically to *Sahih al-Bukhari*—the single most authoritative hadith collection in Sunni Islam, compiled by the ninth-century scholar Muhammad ibn Ismail al-Bukhari after allegedly examining over six hundred thousand traditions and authenticating approximately seven thousand of them. *Sahih al-Bukhari* is organized by topic and fully searchable in English translation, making it accessible to readers with no Arabic background. The collection's rulings on apostasy, blasphemy, the treatment of non-Muslims, the legal status of women, and the prescribed punishments for various offenses are all documented here. Because *Sahih al-Bukhari* carries the highest possible authenticity rating in Sunni jurisprudence—*sahih* meaning rigorously verified—its rulings carry binding legal weight in classical sharia. When this book cites Muhammad's commands, the reader can verify them here directly, in English, without intermediary.

Quranic Resources

Qur'an Gateway *https://www.qurangateway.org*

Qur'an Gateway is the most comprehensive non-devotional academic research platform for the Quran available online—a subscription-based tool developed by Western Quranic scholars and backed by a council of reference comprising leading figures in the field. The platform provides a fully searchable Arabic text of the Quran alongside multiple English translations, advanced linguistic tools including word-by-word morphological parsing and root-based search, and the ability to generate charts and graphs based on user-defined queries—making it possible to analyze patterns across the Quranic text with a precision that no other online tool currently matches. Particularly distinctive is its manuscript module, which includes photographs and detailed descriptions of corrections and variant readings in early Quranic manuscripts—primary source material that illuminates the textual history of the document on which Islamic law is founded. For readers of this book who want not only to read the Quranic verses that underpin classical sharia but to examine the linguistic, textual, and historical dimensions of those verses with scholarly rigor, Qur'an Gateway provides tools that no other resource in this list can match. Available at qurangateway.org and qurangateway.co.uk.

Al-Tafsir.com *https://www.altafsir.com/*

Al-Tafsir.com is the premier online repository of classical Quranic commentary—*tafsir*—in Arabic and, for many works, in English translation. Tafsir is the scholarly discipline of interpreting the Quran, and the classical tafsir works are essential for understanding how Islamic scholars have understood Quranic verses across fourteen centuries. The site hosts the tafsir of Ibn Kathir—the most widely read Quranic commentary in the Sunni world, extensively cited in this book for its interpretation of verses on the jizya, the treatment of non-Muslims, and the legal prescriptions of

Islamic governance—as well as the tafsir of al-Tabari, al-Qurtubi, al-Baghawi, and dozens of other major classical commentators. For readers who want to understand not just what the Quran says but how Islamic legal scholarship has consistently interpreted it over more than a thousand years, this site is an essential resource. The gap between a Quranic verse and its real-world legal application is precisely the gap that tafsir fills—and this site makes that scholarship accessible.

Alim.org—Tafsir Section *https://www.alim.org/tafsir/*

Alim.org offers an integrated platform for Quranic study that combines the Arabic text, multiple English translations, and classical tafsir commentary in a single interface. The tafsir section is particularly useful for readers who want to move between the literal text of the Quran and its authoritative scholarly interpretation without navigating multiple websites. The platform includes the commentary of Ibn Kathir in accessible English translation, cross-referenced with the Quranic text and with relevant hadith—creating a comprehensive study tool that mirrors the method of classical Islamic legal scholarship. For lay readers who want to understand the verses cited throughout this book—Surah 9:29 on the jizya, Surah 5:44 on divine governance, Surah 4:34 on the authority of men over women, Surah 24:2 on the punishment for fornication—Alim.org provides both the text and the scholarly tradition of interpretation that gave those verses their legal force.

SearchTruth.com *https://www.searchtruth.com/*

SearchTruth.com is a comprehensive Islamic reference platform that combines Quranic text, hadith collections, and Islamic reference works in a single searchable interface. The site allows readers to search simultaneously across the Quran, *Sahih al-Bukhari*, *Sahih Muslim*, and other major collections, making it particularly useful for tracing how a specific topic—apostasy, blasphemy, the dhimmi, *hudud* punishments—is treated across multiple primary sources at once. The site also includes Arabic text alongside English translation for readers who want to verify the accuracy of the English rendering against the original. For American readers who want a broad-ranging survey of what the primary sources say on any given topic covered in this book, SearchTruth.com provides an efficient starting point.

Corpus.Quran.com *http://corpus.quran.com/*

The Quranic Arabic Corpus is an academically rigorous linguistic resource that provides morphological and syntactic analysis of every word in the Quran. For readers with some background in Arabic, or for anyone who wants to understand the precise grammatical and lexical meaning of the Arabic terms used in Quranic legislation—*hakimiyya*, *saghirun*, *jizya*, *wilaya*, and others—this site provides word-by-word analysis with grammatical parsing, English glosses, and cross-references to the relevant classical grammatical literature. It is the most linguistically precise Quranic resource available online and is invaluable for anyone who wants to verify that the translations used throughout this book accurately render the Arabic original.

Quran Browser—QB.Gomen.org *http://qb.gomen.org/QuranBrowser/*

The Quran Browser is a multi-translation comparison tool that displays multiple English translations of any Quranic verse side by side, allowing readers to compare how different translators have rendered the same Arabic text. This is particularly useful for the verses cited throughout this book, where the specific wording of the translation—especially in contested passages about the jizya, apostasy, and the treatment of non-Muslims—can significantly affect the reader's understanding. By comparing multiple translations simultaneously, readers can identify where translators agree on the plain meaning of the text and where the range of translations reveals genuine interpretive choices. The Browser includes translations by Abdullah Yusuf Ali, Muhammad Asad, Pickthall, Sahih International, and several others—providing a comprehensive picture of how the Quranic text has been rendered for English-speaking audiences.

Al-Quran.info *https://al-quran.info/#home*

Al-Quran.info is a clean, accessible interface for reading and studying the Quran with side-by-side Arabic text and English translation, audio recitation, and verse-by-verse navigation. The site is designed for accessibility and ease of use, making it an ideal starting point for readers who are encountering the Quranic text for the first time. The platform includes the Sahih

International translation—one of the most widely used and linguistically accurate contemporary English translations—alongside the Arabic original. For readers who want to look up the specific verses cited throughout this book—to read them in their Quranic context rather than in isolated quotation—Al-Quran.info provides a straightforward and reliable tool.

QuranFlash.com *http://www.quranflash.com/home?en*

QuranFlash.com provides a digital reproduction of the Quran in its traditional *mushaf* format—the printed page layout familiar to Muslims worldwide—alongside translation and recitation options. The site is particularly valuable for understanding the Quran as Muslims themselves encounter it in practice: in the physical form in which it is memorized, recited, and studied in Islamic households and institutions around the world. For readers who want to see the Arabic text as it appears in the authoritative printed editions used in Islamic education—the Medina *mushaf* standard—QuranFlash provides that visual experience alongside English navigation tools.

Fatwa and Contemporary Islamic Legal Opinion

IslamQA.info *https://islamqa.info/en*

IslamQA—Islam Question and Answer—is one of the most widely consulted Islamic legal fatwa websites in the world, operated under the supervision of Sheikh Muhammad Salih al-Munajjid, a prominent Saudi scholar in the Salafi tradition. The site answers thousands of questions submitted by Muslims worldwide on every aspect of Islamic law and practice, drawing on the Quran, the hadith, and the rulings of the classical schools. Its importance for this book's argument cannot be overstated: IslamQA represents contemporary, mainstream Salafi Islamic legal opinion—the tradition that is most directly connected to the classical jurisprudence discussed throughout these pages—and its rulings on apostasy, blasphemy, the treatment of non-Muslims, hudud punishments, and the incompatibility of democracy with Islamic governance are exactly what the classical texts say they are. For any reader who wants to verify that the classical rulings described in this book are not merely ancient history but living, contemporary Islamic legal opinion, IslamQA is the most direct evidence available. Search "apostasy," "blasphemy," "jizya," "democracy," or "hudud" and read what contemporary Islamic scholarship, grounded in the classical tradition, actually says.

IslamWeb.net *https://www.islamweb.net/en/*

IslamWeb is a comprehensive Islamic resource portal operated by the Qatar-based organization that provides fatwas, Quranic study tools, hadith databases, and Islamic educational content. The site reflects mainstream contemporary Islamic scholarship from the Gulf tradition—particularly relevant given this book's discussion of Gulf-state funding for Islamist movements in the United States and the West. IslamWeb's fatwa section addresses questions about Islamic law in contemporary contexts, including the application of sharia in non-Muslim-majority societies, the obligations of Muslims living in the West, and the classical rules governing the treatment of non-Muslims. Its accessibility in English makes it a valuable resource for American readers who want to understand how Islamic legal institutions funded by Gulf states present Islamic law to English-speaking Muslim audiences.

Shiʿi Islamic Primary Sources

Thaqalayn.net *https://thaqalayn.net/*

Thaqalayn.net provides access to the major hadith collections of the Twelver Shiʿi tradition—the tradition followed by the majority of Muslims in Iran, Iraq, Lebanon, and Bahrain, and by significant communities in the United States. The site hosts Shiʿi primary texts including *Al-Kafi* of al-Kulayni, *Man La Yahduruhu al-Faqih* of Ibn Babawayh, and *Tahdhib al-Ahkam* of al-Tusi—the four foundational hadith collections of Twelver Shiʿi jurisprudence, analogous in authority to the six major Sunni collections. For readers who want to understand how sharia's incompatibility with the Constitution extends beyond the Sunni tradition to the Shiʿi jurisprudential tradition that governs the Islamic Republic of Iran—the world's most prominent sharia state—Thaqalayn.net provides direct access to the primary sources.

Al-Islam.org *https://al-islam.org/*

Al-Islam.org is the most comprehensive English-language repository of Shiʿi Islamic literature available online, maintained by the Ahlul Bayt Digital Islamic Library Project. The site hosts hundreds of classical and contemporary Shiʿi texts in English translation, including works of theology, jurisprudence, ethics, and history. For the purposes of this book, the site's holdings on Islamic governance, the obligations of the Islamic state, the treatment of non-Muslims, and the political theology of the Imamate are particularly relevant. Al-Islam.org also hosts the works of Ayatollah Khomeini—including his foundational text *Islamic Government* (*Hukumat-e Islami*), which provides the theoretical basis for the Islamic Republic of Iran and represents the most fully implemented modern example of sharia governance—making it essential reading for anyone who wants to understand what sharia-based government looks like in contemporary practice.

PART TWO: CLASSICAL PRIMARY TEXTS

The following classical texts are cited throughout this book and represent the foundational sources of classical sharia jurisprudence. Many are available in English translation in print and through the digital resources listed above.

The Quran

The primary source of Islamic law. Cited throughout in the Sahih International translation. Readers are encouraged to compare multiple translations using the resources listed above, particularly for the legally significant passages in Surah 2, 4, 5, 9, and 24.

Sahih al-Bukhari (Muhammad ibn Ismail al-Bukhari, d. 870 AD)

The most authoritative hadith collection in Sunni Islam. Available in complete English translation at Sunnah.com and Sahih-Bukhari.com. Contains the foundational hadith on apostasy, blasphemy, the treatment of non-Muslims, women's legal status, and the hudud punishments.

Sahih Muslim (Muslim ibn al-Hajjaj, d. 875 AD)

The second most authoritative Sunni hadith collection. Available in English at Sunnah.com. Particularly important for the hadith on stoning, apostasy, and the early Islamic community's treatment of those who left the faith.

Sunan Abu Dawud (Abu Dawud al-Sijistani, d. 889 AD)

One of the six canonical Sunni hadith collections. Contains important traditions on homosexuality, apostasy, and the dhimmi system. Available at Sunnah.com.

Jami al-Tirmidhi (Muhammad ibn Isa al-Tirmidhi, d. 892 AD)

One of the six canonical Sunni hadith collections. Available at Sunnah.com.

Contains traditions on the jizya, treatment of non-Muslims, and the conduct of the early Islamic community.

Tafsir Ibn Kathir (Ismail ibn Kathir, d. 1373 AD)

The most widely read classical Quranic commentary in the Sunni world. Available in English translation at Altafsir.com and Alim.org. Ibn Kathir's commentary on Surah 9:29—the jizya verse—is the definitive classical interpretation of the dhimmi system. His commentary on the legal verses throughout the Quran reflects the mainstream Hanbali jurisprudential tradition.

Tafsir al-Tabari (Muhammad ibn Jarir al-Tabari, d. 923 AD)

The earliest and most comprehensive classical Quranic commentary, preserving the interpretations of the first generations of Islamic scholars. Available in Arabic at Altafsir.com. Essential for understanding how the Quranic legal verses were understood by those closest in time to their revelation.

Minhaj al-Talibin (Yahya ibn Sharaf al-Nawawi, d. 1277 AD)

The foundational legal manual of the Shafi'i school of jurisprudence. Contains the definitive Shafi'i rulings on apostasy, blasphemy, the dhimmi system, and the hudud punishments. Available in English translation in print.

Al-Mughni (Ibn Qudama al-Maqdisi, d. 1223 AD)

The comprehensive legal encyclopedia of the Hanbali school. Contains detailed rulings on apostasy, the treatment of non-Muslims, inheritance, and criminal punishments. Partially available in English translation.

Al-Sarim al-Maslul ala Shatim al-Rasul (Ibn Taymiyya, d. 1328 AD)

"The Drawn Sword Against the One Who Insults the Messenger." Ibn Taymiyya's definitive legal treatise on blasphemy, arguing for the mandatory death penalty for those who insult Muhammad without the possibility of reprieve through repentance. Foundational for contemporary Islamist blasphemy doctrine.

Ighathat al-Lahfan and ***Al-Turuq al-Hukmiyya*** (Ibn Qayyim al-Jawziyya, d. 1350 AD)

Works by Ibn Taymiyya's most distinguished student, extending his mentor's legal analyses on blasphemy, governance, and the treatment of non Muslims. Available in Arabic; partially translated.

Al-Mudawwana al-Kubra (Sahnun ibn Said al-Tanukhi, d. 854 AD)

The foundational legal encyclopedia of the Maliki school, containing the rulings of Imam Malik ibn Anas as transmitted and organized by his students. Contains the Maliki school's rulings on *diya*, testimony, and the dhimmi system.

Mukhtasar Khalil (Khalil ibn Ishaq al-Jundi, d. 1374 AD)

The most concise and widely studied legal manual of the Maliki school. Contains the Maliki rulings on all major areas of Islamic law including the hudud penalties and the treatment of non-Muslims.

Al-Hidaya (Ali ibn Abi Bakr al-Marghinani, d. 1197 AD)

The foundational legal manual of the Hanafi school, the most widely followed school of Sunni jurisprudence globally. Available in English translation as *The Hedaya*. Contains the Hanafi rulings on apostasy, the dhimmi system, and criminal punishments.

Pact of Umar (attributed to the early Islamic caliphate, 7th–8th century AD)

The foundational document establishing the conditions of dhimmi status—the restrictions on church building, public religious expression, dress, housing, and political authority imposed on Christians and Jews under classical

Islamic governance. Available in English translation in multiple online and print sources.

PART THREE: SELECTED SCHOLARLY SECONDARY WORKS

Works by A. S. Ibrahim

The following books represent the author's own scholarly contributions to the study of Islam, its primary texts, its history, and its encounter with Christianity and the West. Each is grounded in the Arabic primary sources examined throughout this book and is written with the dual perspective of an insider—a Coptic Christian who grew up under Islam's cultural dominance—and a trained scholar of Islamic texts and history. Together they constitute the academic foundation from which this book's arguments are drawn.

A.S. Ibrahim. *Muhammad's Military Expeditions.* Oxford University Press, 2024.

This volume represents the author's most recent and most comprehensive scholarly examination of Muhammad's military campaigns as documented in the primary Islamic sources—the *sira* (biographical literature), the hadith collections, and the earliest historical chronicles. Understanding Muhammad's military activity is essential to understanding sharia, because Muhammad's conduct in war—his treatment of conquered peoples, his policies toward apostates and critics, his establishment of the dhimmi system, his prescriptions for the distribution of war spoils including enslaved women—is not incidental to Islamic law. It is its foundation. Whatever Muhammad did is, by definition, the normative Islamic precedent. This book examines those precedents in their historical context and with full scholarly rigor, providing the evidentiary basis for many of the claims made in the present volume about the origins of sharia's most contested doctrines.

A.S. Ibrahim. *Introducing Islam.* Baker Academic, 2020–2024.

Designed as an accessible and authoritative introduction to Islam for Western readers, this three-volume set covers the foundational beliefs, practices, history, and legal tradition of Islam from its origins to the present day. It serves as an ideal companion to the present book for readers who want a comprehensive overview of Islam—its theology, its jurisprudence, its history of expansion, and its encounter with the modern world—before engaging with the specific constitutional conflicts examined here. *Introducing Islam* is grounded in the primary sources and written with the clarity that lay readers require without sacrificing the scholarly precision that the subject demands.

A.S. Ibrahim. *A Concise Guide to Islam.* Baker Academic, 2023.

A compact, accessible reference guide to Islam's beliefs, practices, and legal tradition, designed for readers who want reliable information quickly without academic apparatus. The guide covers the Five Pillars, the six articles of faith, the life of Muhammad, the structure of Islamic law, and Islam's major theological traditions—providing the foundational knowledge that allows readers to engage intelligently with the primary sources and with the arguments of the present volume. It is an ideal starting point for pastors, educators, policy professionals, and any American citizen who wants to understand Islam accurately before forming opinions about its political implications.

A.S. Ibrahim. *Reaching Your Muslim Neighbor with the Gospel.* Crossway, 2022.

Written from the perspective of Christian engagement with Muslim communities, this book provides practical, theologically grounded guidance for Christians who want to share their faith with Muslim neighbors—respectfully, honestly, and with genuine understanding of what Muslims believe and why. The book reflects the author's conviction, expressed throughout the present volume, that opposing Islamism is not the same as opposing Muslims as people, and that the appropriate Christian response to Islam combines clear-eyed theological honesty with genuine love for Muslim individuals. *Reaching Your Muslim Neighbor* is the pastoral complement to the present volume's constitutional analysis—addressing the human and spiritual dimensions of the encounter between Christianity and Islam in America.

A.S. Ibrahim, ed. *Medieval Encounters: Arabic-speaking Christians and Islam.* Gorgias Press, 2022.

This scholarly volume examines the historical encounter between Arabic-speaking Christian communities and the Islamic civilization that surrounded and governed them. Drawing on Arabic Christian primary sources—texts produced in the first three centuries of Islam by Christians who lived under Islamic governance and wrote in the language of their conquerors—the book documents the theological, legal, and cultural dynamics of Christian life under Islamic dominance. It is directly relevant to the present volume's treatment of the dhimmi system, providing historical depth and primary source documentation for the claim that the dhimmi experience described in Chapter Four is not a theoretical construct but a fourteen-century-long historical reality with a rich documentary record. The Arabic-speaking Christians whose voices are recovered in this volume are, in a profound sense, the author's ancestors—and their experience under Islamic governance is one of the formative realities that motivated the writing of this book.

A.S. Ibrahim. *A Concise Guide to the Life of Muhammad.* Baker Academic, 2022.

A scholarly yet accessible biography of Muhammad drawn from the primary Islamic sources—the *sira* literature, the hadith collections, and the early historical chronicles. This guide is indispensable for understanding the present volume because, as emphasized throughout this book, Muhammad's life is not merely the inspiring story of a religious founder. It is the legal template for classical sharia. Everything Muhammad said, did, and approved of is, in Islamic jurisprudence, normative and binding. His ordering of assassinations for those who insulted him, his prescriptions for the treatment of apostates, his establishment of the dhimmi system, his conduct in military campaigns—all of these are documented in this volume from the primary sources and constitute the evidentiary foundation for the legal arguments examined in the present book.

A.S. Ibrahim. *Conversion to Islam.* Oxford University Press, 2021.

Published by one of the world's most prestigious academic presses, this scholarly volume examines the history, theology, and sociology of conversion to Islam—the processes through which individuals and communities have moved into the Islamic faith across fourteen centuries and across the globe. The book is directly relevant to the present volume's treatment of apostasy law because conversion to Islam—the movement into the faith—is the mirror image of apostasy—the movement out of it. Understanding how Islam has historically understood, encouraged, and in some contexts coerced conversion illuminates the mechanisms by which it has maintained and expanded its community and explains the severity of its response to those who reverse that movement. The asymmetry—conversion welcomed, apostasy punished by death—is one of the most revealing structural features of classical sharia's relationship to individual religious freedom.

A.S. Ibrahim. *A Concise Guide to the Quran.* Baker Academic, 2020.

A scholarly and accessible introduction to the Quran—its structure, its history, its major themes, and its relationship to Islamic law and theology—written for Western readers who want to understand Islam's primary sacred text without the barriers of Arabic or specialized academic training. This guide is the essential companion for readers of the present volume who want to engage with the Quranic verses cited throughout these chapters—on divine sovereignty, the jizya, the treatment of women, the hudud penalties, and the status of non-Muslims—in their full textual and theological context. The guide explains how the Quran was compiled, how it is interpreted, and how its legal verses have been understood and applied by Islamic jurisprudence across fourteen centuries. Understanding the Quran as Muslims understand it—not as Western readers might assume it works, but as Islamic tradition has always approached it—is the indispensable foundation for understanding everything this book argues.

A.S. Ibrahim. *The Stated Motivations for the Early Islamic Expansion.* Peter Lang, 2018.

This scholarly monograph examines the primary Islamic sources to reconstruct and analyze the stated motivations that early Muslim leaders and communities articulated for the remarkable military and political expansion of Islam in its first twenty years. Drawing on the *sira*, the hadith, the early chronicles, and the legal literature, the book interrogates the relationship between religious obligation, political ambition, and military strategy in the early Islamic conquests—the conquests that established the *dar al-Islam*, imposed the dhimmi system on the conquered Christian and Jewish populations, and created the political template that classical sharia codified as normative. The book is the scholarly foundation for the present volume's treatment of Islam's inherently expansionist political theology—the *hakimiyya* doctrine, the *dar al-harb / dar al-Islam* framework, and the classical obligation to extend Islamic governance over the world.

Works by Other Scholars

Bat Ye'or. *The Dhimmi: Jews and Christians Under Islam.* Fairleigh Dickinson University Press, 1985.

The definitive historical study of the dhimmi system in practice, drawing on primary sources from across the Islamic world over fourteen centuries. Bat Ye'or's meticulous documentation of the legal, social, and economic conditions of Christian and Jewish communities under Islamic governance provides the historical depth behind Chapter Four's analysis of the dhimmi system's incompatibility with the Fourteenth Amendment.

Bat Ye'or. *Islam and Dhimmitude: Where Civilizations Collide.* Fairleigh Dickinson University Press, 2002.

An examination of how the dhimmi dynamic has evolved into the contemporary political context, tracing the continuities between classical Islamic governance of non-Muslims and the modern experience of Christian and Jewish minorities in Muslim-majority societies.

Andrew Bostom, ed. *The Legacy of Jihad: Islamic Holy War and the Fate of Non-Muslims.* Prometheus Books, 2005.

A comprehensive anthology of primary source documents on the Islamic doctrine of jihad and its historical application to non-Muslim populations, providing essential documentary support for the analysis of Islamic political theology in Chapters One and Six.

Andrew Bostom, ed. *The Legacy of Islamic Antisemitism: From Sacred Texts to Solemn History.* Prometheus Books, 2008.

A documentary history of Islamic jurisprudence and practice regarding Jews, drawing on primary sources from the Quran, hadith, and classical fiqh to establish the historical depth and doctrinal consistency of the legal hierarchies described in Chapter Four.

Nonie Darwish. *Cruel and Usual Punishment: The Terrifying Global Implications of Islamic Law.* Thomas Nelson, 2008.

A firsthand account by an Egyptian-American former Muslim of the human reality of sharia governance, combined with rigorous analysis of its legal structure. Darwish's inside perspective—shaped, like the author's, by direct experience of Islamic cultural dominance in Egypt—gives this book a credibility and urgency that purely academic treatments cannot match.

Ayaan Hirsi Ali. *Infidel.* Free Press, 2007.

The memoir of a Somali-born former Muslim who experienced Islamic governance firsthand and became one of its most articulate and courageous critics in the West. Hirsi Ali's account of her journey from Islamic observance to secular freedom—and of the death threats and institutional hostility she faced for making that journey publicly—is one of the most powerful personal testimonies to the human cost of the doctrines examined in this book.

Paul Marshall, Lela Gilbert, and Nina Shea. *Persecuted: The Global Assault on Christians.* Thomas Nelson, 2013.

A comprehensive, rigorously documented account of the persecution of Christian minorities under Islamic governance across the Middle East, Africa, and Asia—providing the contemporary evidentiary basis for the historical patterns described in Chapter Four and in the Preface.

Nina Shea and Paul Marshall. *Silenced: How Apostasy and Blasphemy Codes Are Choking Freedom Worldwide.* Oxford University Press, 2011.

A detailed examination of apostasy and blasphemy laws in Muslim-majority countries, with extensive documentation of their human cost—providing essential contemporary evidence for the constitutional arguments made in Chapters Two and Three.

Sayyid Qutb. *Milestones (Ma'alim fi al-Tariq).* Various editions.

The foundational manifesto of modern Islamist political theology, arguing that all contemporary societies are in a state of *jahiliyya* and that the obligation of Muslims is to establish Islamic governance based on divine sovereignty. Understanding Qutb is essential to understanding the ideological foundations of every major Islamist movement operating in the United States today, and this book should be read—with clear eyes and full awareness of its implications—by every American who wants to understand what political Islam actually seeks.

Ayatollah Ruhollah Khomeini. *Islamic Government (Hukumat-e Islami).* Available at Al-Islam.org.

The theoretical foundation of the Islamic Republic of Iran, representing the most fully implemented modern example of sharia governance and the clearest documentary evidence of what divine sovereignty looks like when it is given state power. Available online at Al-Islam.org and essential reading for anyone who wants to move from the theoretical arguments of Chapter Six to their real-world institutional expression.

Sayyid Abul Ala Mawdudi. *Towards Understanding Islam* and related works. Various editions.

The foundational works of the Pakistani Islamist scholar who coined the modern political use of *hakimiyya* and who developed the most systematic argument for Islam's incompatibility with democracy. Mawdudi's influence on contemporary Islamist movements worldwide—from the Muslim Brotherhood to the organizations operating in the United States today—makes his writings essential reading for understanding the ideological tradition this book engages.

www.ingramcontent.com/pod-product-compliance
Lightning Source LLC
LaVergne TN
LVHW050934210926
848482LV00013B/607